Markt- und Unternehmensentwicklung
Markets and Organisations

Edited by

A. Picot, München, Deutschland
R. Reichwald, Leipzig, Deutschland
E. Franck, Zürich, Schweiz
K. M. Möslein, Erlangen-Nürnberg, Deutschland

Change of institutions, technology and competition drives the interplay of markets and organisations. The scientific series 'Markets and Organisations' addresses a magnitude of related questions, presents theoretic and empirical findings and discusses related concepts and models.

More information about this series at http://www.springer.com/series/12561

Hari Suman Naik

Simplifying Solution Space

Enabling Non-Expert Users to Innovate and Design with Toolkits

With a foreword by Prof. Dr. Kathrin M. Möslein

Springer Gabler

Hari Suman Naik
Nürnberg, Germany

Dissertation Friedrich-Alexander-Universität Erlangen-Nürnberg / 2016

Markt- und Unternehmensentwicklung Markets and Organisations
ISBN 978-3-658-18282-3 ISBN 978-3-658-18283-0 (eBook)
DOI 10.1007/978-3-658-18283-0

Library of Congress Control Number: 2017940468

Springer Gabler

Printed on acid-free paper

This Springer Gabler imprint is published by Springer Nature
The registered company is Springer Fachmedien Wiesbaden GmbH
The registered company address is: Abraham-Lincoln-Str. 46, 65189 Wiesbaden, Germany

Foreword

From individual artisans to assembly line standardization to user innovation and design, production has come full circle. New technologies like digital fabrication and advancements in electronics give users a large solution space to innovate and design solutions that match their heterogeneous and sticky needs. Extant research has shown that appropriate toolkits can assist users in articulating their needs. For non-expert users, this is best achieved when the solution space is simplified without sacrificing design flexibility. Dr. Hari Suman Naik's work builds on and advances existing research in the use of toolkits and their design. It addresses the fundamental research problem of how toolkit solution space can be simplified to enable non-expert users, with a much-needed perspective of modular systems.

His unique work is structured in the form of three studies on toolkit solution space that address the three aspects of an artifact: namely the use (outer), the structure (inner), and the design (interface). The first two studies build on case study research to qualitatively explore, how solution space is simplified from the user's and the toolkit's side respectively. These explorative studies identify mechanisms for managing the complexity of the solution space among users and within toolkits. The mechanisms provide the foundation for the third study that designs and evaluates a toolkit artifact at the interface between the outer and inner environments.

By covering these three aspects, the thesis overcomes the ever-lurking danger of a rift developing between knowledge on the use of toolkits in innovation activities and the design of toolkits, which naturally co-exist, thereby achieving stimulating results. Solution space can be simplified by starting with minimal designs using only the necessary solution space and then iterating towards more complexity. Modularity enables non-expert users to share the design workload with other users or reuse existing designs. Building dynamic interfaces (both physical and informational) can support reusing existing designs. The use of algorithms to generate and recommend complete solutions also emerges as a promising approach that is convincingly demonstrated and evaluated.

Hari's work clearly delivers significant advancement in knowledge on toolkits and user innovation and provides especially fruitful and valuable contributions towards understanding and designing the toolkit solution space. It is a fascinating and bold work on state-of-the-art technological advancements, based on sound, and established theory. The book deserves broad dissemination both in the research community and in management practice. It is especially recommended to innovation managers interested in bringing toolkit-based user innovation to their organizations. Users who have a strong urge to materialize their creativity and solve problems, but consider themselves non-experts can also rejoice.

This book is a much-needed travel guide to traverse the innovation solution space!

Prof. Dr. Kathrin M. Möslein

Preface

This book is my first, and like other books that are doctoral dissertations, it is a result of a sustained effort, alongside a period of self-discovery and self-development. The tremendous potential in the fields of innovation management and information systems motivated me to aim for a trailblazing topic. This ambition tempered over time through constant discussions on structuring and presenting my ideas. These discussions also helped me assimilate various aspects of living in Germany, my current home, so I could enjoy its reliability and not feel too isolated. I learned to enjoy this initially unfamiliar environment through commitment and patience and subsequently developed many new skills and myself.

I have a deep appreciation towards those who encouraged and persisted with me during my dissertation quest. I thank my colleagues (who are now friends) and my advisor for including me in their social and research circles, sparring ideas with me, and for evaluating my work. They taught me to structure my writing and in turn structure my thinking. The more experienced researchers among them acted as valuable mentors and the others a constant stream of much needed fresh thoughts. I am also grateful to all those who participated in this research. Their inspiring work has provided invaluable insights, which this book has sought to capture and convey.

Most of all, thank you, Anja. You have shared the weight of my expectations and weathered my whimsical fits. Having you around made this challenge much easier to overcome!

Overview of Contents

Table of Contents

List of Figures

List of Tables

List of Abbreviations

AMCIS	American Conference of Information Systems
CAS	Computer-aided design
CRS	Constraint-based Recommender Systems
DSR	Design Science Research
FIRST	Feedback-based IteRative Solutions Toolkit
GPL	General Public License
ICIS	International Conference of Information Systems
ICT	Information and Communication Technologies
IoT	Internet of Things
KRS	Knowledge-based Recommender Systems
MVC	Model-view-controller
OPAC	Online Public Access catalog
RS	Recommender Systems
STL	Standard Triangle Language/Standard Tessellation Language
STL	Stereolithography
TC	Traditional Customizer Toolkit

Part I

Introduction:

Solution Space for User Innovation and Design

1 The Challenge of Simplifying Solution Space

Innovation occurs when better solutions emerge that meet existing, new or newly identified market needs (Maranville, 1992). It can arise through novelty in either solution information or need information or both. Users of products and services, whether they use these products and service professionally as part of firms, or as end consumers are increasingly able to innovate and design from both ends of the need-solution spectrum (von Hippel, 2005). Users often develop a sound knowledge of their individual needs and sometimes the needs of other users close to them, i.e., due to connections at a personal or professional level (von Hippel, 1994). As they use a product or a service available to them in the market, they have to a certain degree, made a conscious decision of choosing the solution that is closest to meeting their needs. However, often as is the case, the available solutions may only partly satisfy their needs, or may not exist.

Some users are capable of providing solutions or at least parts of solutions that meet their needs. In some of these cases, the users have solution ideas, and they have access to essential capabilities such as skills, tools, and technologies to convert their ideas into finished solutions. In other cases, users have great ideas for new solutions, but their solution information is incomplete without production capabilities. In these cases, they collaborate with manufacturers or other users with these production capabilities and together come up with new solutions (Prahalad & Ramaswamy, 2004). Manufacturing firms benefit from this phenomenon of user contribution at both ends of the need-solution spectrum. They can:

1. Benefit by communicating to users who have need information and then providing innovative (new or better) solutions that meet their needs (Urban & von Hippel, 1988).
2. Collaboratively develop new or better solutions with users and offer them to the market (Kambil, Friesen, & Sundaram, 1999).
3. Acquire completed solutions from users, optimize them, and add them to their portfolio (von Hippel & Katz, 2002).

The various methods that firms can use to interact with users and benefit from their need and solution information differ vastly in their scope and effectiveness. For example, firms can have an initial market survey and find out some more about their user needs or have a series of co-creation workshops (Piller, Ihl, Vossen, & Group, 2011) and get access to in-depth needs and, to some extent, solution information. However, these methods lead to interaction costs that limit how extensively firms can use them. Often, firms use these methods to interact with samples of users whom they assume represent users with need or solution information.

One method for lowering the interaction costs is by using toolkits for user innovation and design (von Hippel, 2001). Toolkits are systems (often information systems) that manufacturers can offer to every user. The term "toolkits for user innovation and design" encompasses systems that efficiently perform either of the following interactions[1] in a cost effective way (Franke & Piller, 2004; Franke & Schreier, 2002):

1. Transfer users' need information to the manufacturer and the manufacturer's solution information to the user (design or customization).
2. Enable users to extend solution information from the manufacturer based on their needs (user innovation).

The first interaction mentioned above is present in *toolkits for customizing* products or services to fit users' needs rather than innovating new solutions, say for example a toolkit where users can design their custom eyeglasses (von Hippel, 2001). In the case of electronic or informational products, firms can easily offer a product that the user can customize by providing configurable options. Such options are almost ubiquitous in today's software with nearly every product having a 'Settings' option through which the product can be customized to suit the user's needs better. Here the firm

---

[1] A third interaction is also possible with toolkits for idea competitions (TIC) that transfer more generic ideas containing partial need and solution information from users to manufacturers (Piller & Walcher, 2006). Chapter 3 explains why TICs are different from toolkits for user innovation and design. Hence, this chapter omits the interaction.

offers the user a set of solution options from which the user may select the best fitting options to their otherwise unmet need. A case study of Apache security software revealed how such toolkits satisfied heterogeneous needs in digital products (Franke & von Hippel, 2003).

In the case of purely physical products, instances of configurable material products are perhaps relatively lesser, but still considerably many. An example is of configurable furniture and lighting systems that users can after purchase (Gilmore & Pine, 1997). The concept is widespread as products become more complex such as in mountain bikes, medical equipment, automobiles, etc. where users may also experience changing needs or the needs change when the product is used by different users (Zipkin, 1997). While this is a great approach to provide a range of solution information to the user, the design of the product restricts the solution range.

Firms can also offer a wider range of solutions to users through the flexibility of their manufacturing processes, design, and technologies. Due to advances in manufacturing processes and technologies, firms can be more flexible in their solution offerings as they can create individualized products at mass production efficiency. These advances marked the shift from mass production to mass customization in manufacturing (Tseng & Jiao, 1996). Firms offer this type of mass-customization to users through internet based software toolkits, where users can specify their needs and can order their customized products. Examples include configurators provided by Dell (customized laptops) or Nike (customized shoes). Further examples can be found at the Configurator Database, one of the biggest online data collections of configurators with more than 1000 entries listed and categorized in 16 different industries (Cyledge, 2014). Figure 1 and its associated box explain the Sake set Creator from Shapeways, one of the newer examples of such toolkits for customized products.

The second interaction is present in *toolkits for innovation,* where users can in a cost effective manner design innovative solutions. While manufacturers use the earlier examples of toolkits to offer users an understood or known set of solutions, these toolkits enable users to develop solutions, of which the manufacturer is unaware. The toolkits provide one part of the solution information while the user develops the rest based on the user's need information (Thomke & Von Hippel, 2002). Such toolkits are appropriate when the need information is "sticky" i.e. it is not easily transferrable from users to firms, making it easier to equip these users to develop solutions themselves (von Hippel, 2001). These toolkits were initially documented and conceptualized by von Hippel as "Toolkits for User Innovation" from his study on the semiconductor and electronics industry (von Hippel, 2001). While they allow users to design new solutions, they do not outsource all the design work to the users. Instead, they have modules of embedded design knowledge that users can utilize to innovate on their own, according to their specific needs. Von Hippel mentions LSI Logic, which released its tools to design innovative circuits to customers and as a result revolutionized the semiconductor industry. Another example is Nestle that released a recipe toolkit based on combinable modules of different taste-flavors. Various informational products come with additional features, meant for users to create previously unforeseen solutions. For example, desktop computer operating systems and smartphone operating systems come with additional development kits for users to make additional software (Kankanhalli, Ye, & Teo, 2015). Similarly, computer games provide kits for users to develop levels, scenarios and characters resulting in novel gameplay and user experiences (L. Jeppesen, 2003; L. B. Jeppesen, 2005; L. B. Jeppesen & Molin, 2003; Piller, Ihl, Füller, Stotko, & Ag, 2004; Prügl & Schreier, 2006). These toolkits targetted "lead users" whose current needs predict future needs in the marketplace (von Hippel, 2001).

Although users can create new solutions, there are clear bounds on the solutions available to users when using a toolkit. The bounds outline the range of solutions, also called a toolkit's "solution space." As von Hippel explained with the example of semiconductor toolkits, the toolkit gave users a solution space restricted to any possible connections between pre-defined logic elements. This flexibility was enough to build different types of computer processors but cannot be used to design bicycles or houses (von Hippel, 2001).

In the case of physical products, the flexibility of the underlying production process limits toolkit solution space. The flexibility has vastly increased due to advances in manufacturing as well as information and communication systems. However, despite having this production flexibility, manufacturers have to be careful with the diversity of solutions they offer. Too much solution space may lead to unforeseen costs from

Sake Set Creator from Shapeways: The Sake Set Creator from Shapeways is one of their first 3D printing customization toolkits. As the name suggests, it creates crockery that is themed after the Japanese tradition of drinking Sake. The toolkit allows users to design sake set items by modifying a default design in two ways. Users can change the position of certain points that denote the planar cross-section of the object. The toolkit generates a cylindrically symmetric 3D design by extrapolating the points along the vertical axis. The other way is by modifying the smoothness of the surface and the twist in the pattern. The toolkit uses a 3D renderer so that users get instant feedback for their modifications and can visualize the object. Figure 1 shows a screenshot of the toolkit.

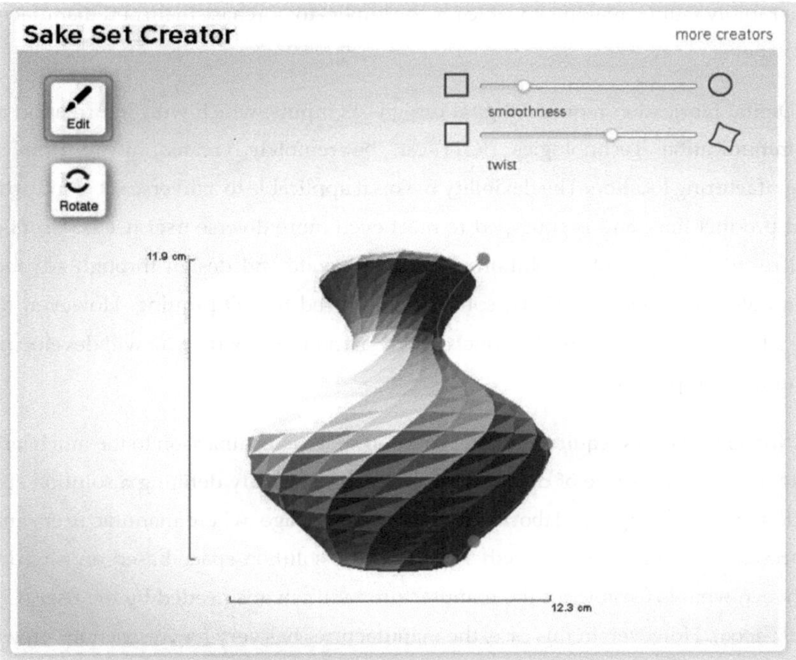

Figure 1: Screen shot of Sake Set Creator

high component variety, a large number of suppliers and high administrative complexity. Irregular customer needs also make it difficult to plan production and can lead to resource shortages or under-utilization (Chen, Wang, & Tseng, 2009).

Over the years, new technologies have emerged that promise to add even more flexibility to production processes, already seen through mass customization strategies. New technologies have promoted *digital fabrication*, from *automated machining tools* to create any shape out of a base material by drilling or milling (subtracting) operations to *additive manufacturing techniques* such as *3D printing* and *laser sintering*. Digital fabrication gives users the freedom to design items in almost any 3D shape imaginable in a variety of materials such as plastics, glass, ceramic, metal, etc. (Dimitrov, Schreve, & Beer, 2006). These systems are rapidly improving, in terms of new functionalities[2], build quality, build sizes, reliability, materials, and they are poised to take over many traditional production systems in the near future (Brody & Pureswaran, 2013).[3] Furthermore, the costs and size of the fabrication equipment are also rapidly falling, making it viable for consumers to purchase them and manufacture at home.

Digital fabrication requires digital designs as inputs, which with Information and Communication Technologies (ICT) can be remotely created, away from the manufacturing location. The flexibility makes it applicable to a diverse set of industries and product lines and is equipped to meet even more diverse user needs. Users can utilize this vast potential solution space to innovate and design through advanced Computer-aided Design (CAD) software optimized for 3D printing. However, they are all-purpose tools for professionals and restricted to experts who will develop new solutions completely.

Non-expert users require a smaller solution space in comparison to the much larger potential solution space of digital fabrication. Traditionally defining a solution space is done by following a collaborative configuration stage, where manufacturers and a representative set of users together develop the solution space based on a tradeoff between what is feasible for the manufacturer and what is needed by the user (Chen et al., 2009). However, in this case, the manufacturer has very few restrictions on what

---

[2] Voxel8 is a 3D electronics printers combines thermoplastics with conductive silver ink to print objects with electronic circuitry. It enables 3D stacking of electronics in a way previously impossible.

[3] IBM expects 3D printing, intelligent robotics, and open source electronics will produce an average 23 percent unit cost benefit and reduce entry barriers by 90 percent.

is feasible, and the users' needs can be too heterogeneous to capture by interacting with just a few sampled users. Furthermore, non-expert users will also need a specially defined solution space that allows them to extend solution information, without having to design everything from scratch. This requirement contrasts with the previous example of a toolkit for custom integrated circuits, where the need related part of solution information could easily be separated and handed over to users (von Hippel, 2001; von Hippel & Katz, 2002).

These issues with large solution spaces lead to the *challenge of simplifying solution space*, as new design freedoms these technologies present uncover the problem of developing appropriate toolkit solution spaces out of the much larger potential solution space. This problem of developing toolkit solution space, opening its development to users (Helminen, Ainoa, & Mäkinen, 2015) and democratizing it for non-expert users has been under-researched in user innovation and design literature (Goduscheit & Jørgensen, 2013; Salvador, Holan, & Piller, 2009). Hence the research question for this dissertation is:

How can toolkit solution space be simplified to enable non-expert users for user innovation and design?

This dissertation strives to provide these insights and set forth new research directions in this upcoming field. The overall objective here is to explore and design solution space simplification. i.e., mechanisms that currently exist to simplify solution space for non-expert users and to design improved mechanisms to do so. The empirical context of the dissertation is user innovation related to digital fabrication, which exhibits large solution spaces. The overall research question of the dissertation is broken down into three sub-research questions:

RQ1: How do users simplify their solution space to create innovative solutions?

RQ2: How do toolkits for user innovation and design simplify solution space for non-expert users?

RQ3: Can a toolkit that generates recommendations simplify solution space and enable non-expert users?

The objectives of the three sub-research questions are:

1) *User perspective on simplifying solution space:* The solution space of digital fabrication technologies like 3D printing is the solution space of *one* of many technologies accessible to users. Innovative users access multiple solution spaces based on multiple technologies to make innovative artifacts. Therefore, it is important to explore how users innovate, design new products using many such solution spaces, and identify mechanisms for simplifying it for non-expert users. It includes systematically formulating the development of new solution information by user innovators and identifying techniques or mechanisms that helped them in this process.
2) *Toolkit perspective on simplifying solution space:* After exploring the simplification of solution space by users using multiple toolkits, the next objective is to systematically study toolkit solution space and explore how toolkits simplify it in their design. Exploring toolkit solution space is crucial to understand its structure and identify mechanisms for future toolkits to adopt. Future studies can use the systematic categorization of solution space as a framework for analyzing solution spaces in this context.
3) *Design perspective on simplifying solution space:* Designing artifacts based on the mechanisms identified in explorative studies and evaluating them can further substantiate the current mechanisms for simplifying solution space. The objective is to develop unique artifacts, which can leverage technology to solve the research problem and to evaluate them in a controlled setting, thus allowing theorizing on the interaction between users and toolkits and its effects.

Thus, with the challenge of toolkit solution space, the research question and the objectives of the dissertation outlined, it moves on to the next chapter, which discusses the relevant theory used in this dissertation that aligns to the research questions and provides the necessary framing for its studies.

2 Framing for the Dissertation

Toolkits for user innovation and design are artifacts, i.e. they fall in the realm of the artificial or 'man-made' as opposed to being natural. According to Simon (1969), artifacts are outputs of engineering activity or skill. They are designed or synthesized to have certain desired properties. This definition applies to toolkits and their solution space as well. They are products of what they ought to be, to attain their goals and to function (Simon, 1969).

2.1 Characteristics of Artifacts

Artifacts have a purpose or function, and the fulfillment of this purpose involves a relation among three aspects: 1) the purpose or goal of the artifact, 2) the structure of the artifact and 3) the environment in which the artifact performs. Two of these three aspects, the structure of the artifact itself and the environment in which it performs are concerned with *how things are*. The purpose or goal of the artifact, on the other hand, is concerned with *how things ought to be* (Simon, 1969). For example, the design of toolkit solution space depends on how 1) the internal structure of the solution space and 2) the context of its use should be brought together to meet its goals.

Simon also describes an artifact as an "interface" between an "inner" environment, the substance, and organization of the artifact itself, and an "outer" environment, the surroundings in which it operates. The artifact will have served its intended purpose when it appropriately matches both the inner and outer environments of the artifact. Such a perspective has an advantage of predicting an artifact's behavior only based on the artifact's goals, its outer environment, and only a minimal knowledge of its inner environment. The rest of the inner working of the artifact is largely irrelevant to predict behavior. The artifact can thus be considered a "black box." The term comes from the auto industry where automakers do the basic engineering such as the exterior, interface structure, goal-related performance specifications while the suppliers do the rest of the detailed engineering (Clark, Chew, Fujimoto, Meyer, & Scherer, 1987).

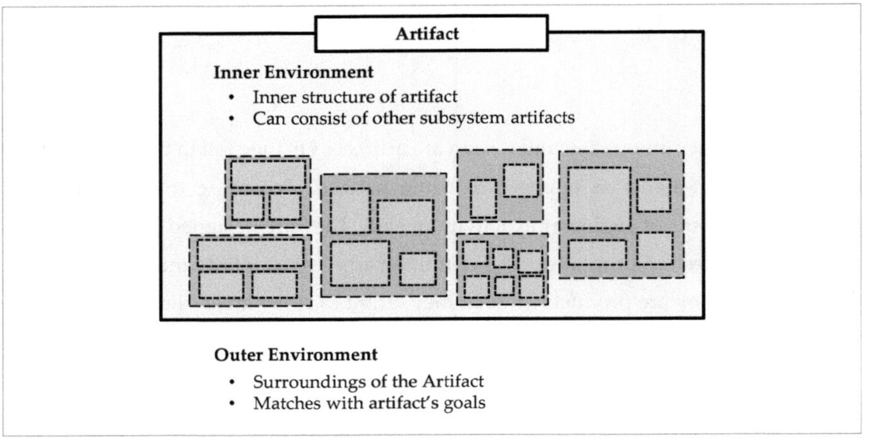

Figure 2: Artifacts as an interface based on Simon (1969)

The inner environment of the artifact can consist of other artifacts that in turn have their inner environments, making an artifact a hierarchical system[4] composed of interrelated subsystems (Simon, 1969). The abstraction of the artifact leads to its recursive or iterative nature, a recurring theme in the dissertation. Figure 2 depicts this view of artifacts, which shows an artifact and its inner and outer environments. Such hierarchical systems exhibit organized complexity (Weaver, 1948) and they can be better understood by analyzing their 'decomposability.' A nearly decomposable system is one in which interactions among subsystems are weak, but not necessarily negligible (Simon, 1969). Designing an artifact so that it has reduced interactions between its subsystems has some advantages, which the below section explains.

2.2 Modularity in Products

Theory on modularity follows the perspective of nearly decomposable systems. Modular systems are special system architectures where the system design is intentionally created with a high degree of loose coupling between components, using

[4] The word hierarchy here refers to an ordered relationship between the system and subsystems rather than lines of defined authority as seen in formal hierarchies in organizations.

standardized interfaces. Product components with standardized interfaces make them almost independent, such that a *change* in the design of one component has little effect on the design of other components in the product (Sanchez & Mahoney, 1996). Modular product architecture is flexible and allows substitution by a range of components, especially when components have gone beyond their life cycle or need to be upgraded by successive component generations (Garud & Kumaraswamy, 1993; Ulrich, 1995).

An often-mentioned example of a modular design architecture is the personal computer. It has loosely coupled components such as microprocessors, disk drives, and peripherals. A manufacturer can substitute each of these components with altered designs without redesigning the other components. Substitution can happen either higher up or lower down the hierarchy of subsystems. Substituting the lowest subsystems is associated with refining or extending the product while substituting higher subsystems are associated with more dramatic deviations from established core concepts and call forth new skills and resources (Clark, 1985).

From an engineering perspective, a modularization has three purposes: 1) to make complexity manageable, 2) to enable parallel work and 3) to accommodate future uncertainty. User innovation and design demonstrate these three aspects of modularity. A toolkit for users to design innovative products or the product that is developed exhibits modularity in its solution space (von Hippel, 2001). A system where users can mix-and-match elements to come up with a product that suits their needs exhibits *modularity-in-use*. For example, using the personal computer example earlier, a toolkit can allow users to select the appropriate modules of microprocessors, disk drives, and peripherals ideal for their needs. Through a toolkit, users contribute to the design of the product, where they design certain modules while the firms design the other modules of the product. This form of modularity is referred to as *modularity-in-design,* and it is explained further in the next section (Baldwin & Clark, 2004).

2.3 Modularity in Organizations

While organizations typically design products, modular product designs can lead to products that design organizations as well, transforming rigid, centralized organizational structures to flexible modular organizational structures (Sanchez & Mahoney, 1996). Such a transformation is possible because a modular product architecture can lead to modularization in the development processes. Traditional design approaches emphasized optimization and led to tightly integrated product designs that required processes with intensive managerial coordination. On the other hand, standardized component interfaces in a modular product architecture enable breaking down the development activities of these components and carrying them out separately, by means of an embedded coordination of development activities. Such modularity can be in the form of *modularity-in-production* where different production sites manufacture products or components, and they later assembled. In the special case where the process of design itself can be split up across separate modules, it is in the form of *modularity-in-design* (Baldwin & Clark, 2004).

Modularity brings in a reduction in managerial authority needed to coordinate development processes. It leads to both concurrent and autonomous development of components, by loosely coupled organizational structures (Orton & Weick, 1990). A multidivisional firm, for example, has tasks that require low levels of coordination and hence can be carried out by divisions that are loosely coupled to each other (Weick, 1976). Modular divisions can also extend across organizations and lay down the architecture of the industry. It sets the framework within which competition will occur and develop (Abernathy & Clark, 1985).

Modularity in organizations allows firms to specialize in the competencies they need to perform their development processes. In user innovation, users and firms carry out development processes together. Hence, the modularity perspective is also applicable to processes conducted through coordination between users (also in communities) and firms. The solution space of users to innovate thus depends on the module of design to which they contribute. Heterogeneity of user needs, a key aspect of user innovation, is a driver of modularity (Schilling, 2000). Environmental pressures in the form of increased competition from online sales, technological change and creation of standards in electronics design and communication technologies act as a catalyst to this phenomenon.

User designed products display modularity-in-design as both firms and users design separate modules of the product. Toolkit solution space specifies the design rules that coordinate these modules, rather than through ongoing consultations between the firm and users. Modularity-in-design allows the creation of new design options, which have associated option value. It makes product design more flexible and increases the total economic value of the system (Baldwin & Clark, 2004).

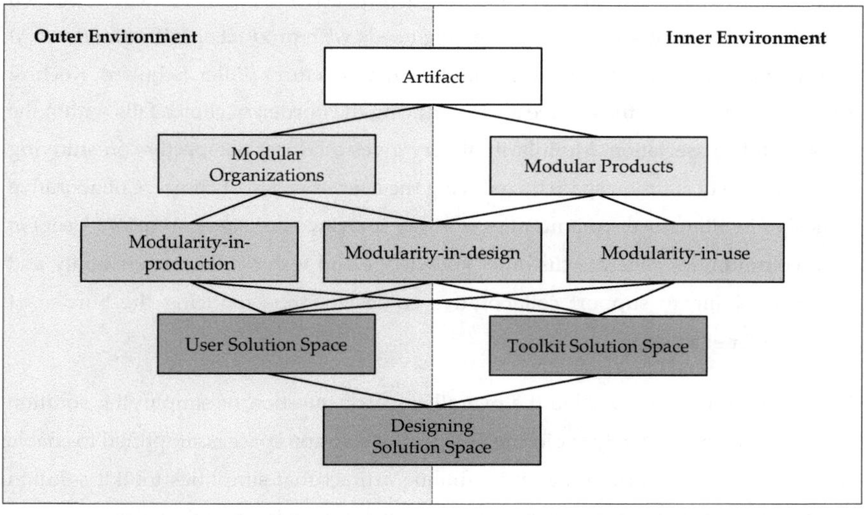

Figure 3: Theoretical framing of modularity used in the dissertation

2.4 Modularity for Simplifying Solution Space

Figure 3 summarizes the theoretical framing of the dissertation explained in the previous sections of the chapter. It also connects the theories to the three-sub research questions explained in the previous chapter that leads to the three studies of the dissertation. The different forms of modularity act as a theoretical lens for exploring how users simplify their solution space and how toolkits simplify solution space. The dissertation uses both modularity in products and modularity in organizations as theoretical perspectives. These perspectives along with the findings from the exploratory studies guide the design of the toolkit artifact, which generates solutions as it lies at the interface between the outer and inner environments.

A modular design reduces complexity as users only have to design their component instead of the whole design and hence it simplifies solution space. However, within the design space of a user's component, numerous options to "mix-and-match" modules can still be overwhelming. Studies in mass-customization toolkits, which follow a modular design show that users face a mass-confusion effect when being presented with too many options (Huffman & Kahn, 1998). Sources of mass confusion from the user's perspective can be categorized into the following three areas: 1) burden of choice due to excess variety, 2) matching needs with product specifications and 3) information gap regarding the behavior of the manufacturer (Piller, Schubert, Koch, & Möslein, 2005). Out of these three areas, reducing the burden of choice falls within the scope of this dissertation. Modularity theory gives a critical perspective on studying simplification of solution space by reducing the user's burden of choice. Collaborative co-design in online user communities is a way to overcome mass-confusion. Users in these communities generate customer knowledge and foster collective creativity and problem solving to support collaborative co-design, thus reducing the burden of choice (Piller et al., 2005).

The dissertation aims to solve the overall research question of simplifying solution space by both qualitatively exploring how toolkit solution space is simplified to enable non-expert users and by designing a unique artifact that simplifies toolkit solution space using the explorative studies. The designed artifact is a toolkit that assists users in their decision-making process and thereby reduces the burden of choice. Using recommender systems is a recognized approach to assist users' decision-making process, by recommending them certain options that better fit their needs (Resnick & Varian, 1997). The artifact designed in this dissertation automates the design process, generates complete solutions, and recommends a sample set of solutions from which users select solutions that meet their needs. It uses knowledge of recommender systems to reduce the search process and simplify solution space for the user.

Thus, artifacts and modularity are the underlying theories that frame this dissertation. The next chapter will establish definitions of key terms used in the studies. A brief structure of the dissertation follows right after and together, the four chapters of *Part I* set up the foundation for the three studies.

3 Definitions of Significant Terms

Literature and everyday language use the notion of "solution space" and "toolkits" quite often to describe varying concepts and ideas, resulting in ambiguous interpretations of these phrases. This chapter strictly defines these key terms for the purpose of this dissertation. To begin, von Hippel coined the term "Toolkits for user innovation" and defined them as:

> *"a coordinated set of user-friendly design tools that enable users to develop new product innovations for themselves (…) they are specific to the design challenges of a specific field or subfield, such as integrated circuit design or software product design."* (von Hippel & Katz, 2002, p. 821)

He emphasized that toolkits for user innovation be considered different from systems used for mass-customization as:

> *"They will also provide the 'design side' that is currently missing for users and producers of mass-customized products. In effect, user toolkits for innovation can provide users with true design freedom – as opposed to the mere opportunity to choose from lists of options that is currently offered by mass-customizers."* (von Hippel, 2001, p. 248)

However, the introduction of the term "toolkits for user innovation and design" expanded upon the previous definition and included toolkits that lead to product adaptations and individualization, in addition to toolkits for user innovation.

> *"Not all toolkits allow for radically new products. Specifically, in consumer markets, there are also toolkits where the focus is not so much on radical innovations (as opposed to high-end toolkits) as on product adaptation and individualization. Users equipped with these low-end design toolkits build their own unique products"* (Franke & Schreier, 2002, p. 9)

Including systems for individualization into the definition makes sense, as it is problematic to absolutely state that product adaptations have no true design freedom. Other forms of toolkits have emerged in innovation management literature over the years, such as "toolkits for open innovation" (Piller et al., 2004), "communities-based toolkits" (L. B. Jeppesen & Molin, 2003) and "toolkits for idea competitions" (Piller & Walcher, 2006). These are interesting variations but dilute the meaning of toolkits used in this dissertation.

In this dissertation, toolkits refer to systems that follow the objectives stated by von Hippel. Toolkits allow users to learn through performing cycles of trial-and-error. Secondly, they offer users a 'solution space' of design freedom not exceeding the manufacturer's production capabilities. Thirdly, well-designed toolkits are user-friendly enough to enable their competitive use without additional training. Fourthly, they will contain libraries of standard modules that function as a starting point for their design changes. Fifthly, properly designed toolkits will ensure that the manufacturer can produce user-designed products or services without requiring any further revisions (von Hippel & Katz, 2002). Hence, the dissertation defines toolkits as:

> ***Toolkits for User Innovation and Design (UID):*** *Toolkits for UID are modular systems for users to innovate and design completed solutions based on their needs, by performing learning cycles of trial-and-error.*

The dissertation refers to the term solution space in two ways. First, it can refer to the solution space of the toolkit, defined by the toolkit maker chosen out of the larger potential solution space of the production system.

> *"(…) the preexisting capability and degrees of freedom built into a given manufacturer's production system"* (von Hippel & Katz, 2002, p. 826)

From the user perspective, a user can use multiple products and services and multiple toolkits for the user's innovation and design goals. It leads to the second definition of the term solution space, where the solution space of the user is the *combined* set of solution spaces of the various toolkits used. This definition is in contrast to solution space in creativity and design literature (e.g. as is seen in Dorst and Cross (2001)), where solution space refers to solution ideas and is unrelated to available toolkits. Hence, the dissertation proposes the following definitions it uses for solution space:

Solution Space of a Toolkit: *Solution Space is the flexibility and freedom of a toolkit bounded by the capability and degrees of freedom in the underlying production system and product architecture.*

Solution Space of a User: *Solution Space is the flexibility and freedom a user has when using a toolkit or a set of toolkits to design based on the user's needs.*

Baldwin and Clark (Baldwin & Clark, 2004) propose modularity as a means to handle complexity. Analyzing empirical data through the lens of modularity theory achieves "*simplifying*" in the context of this dissertation. They define complexity regarding knowledge and effort measured by the capacity of a human being as a "natural unit." An artifact moves from simple to complex when 1) a single person can no longer make it, and 2) a single person can no longer comprehend it. The former requires the division of labor to simplify it, while the latter requires a distribution of knowledge and effort that goes into the design (Baldwin & Clark, 2001).

This thesis separates novice users or non-expert users from expert users. Non-expert users have no specific knowledge and cannot understand all the aspects of the product. Hence they rely on learning-by-doing cycles (von Hippel & Katz, 2002) of the toolkit to develop solution information. Although users possess need information, it may also be in an in implicit form (Kujala, 2002; von Hippel & von Krogh, 2013) and users discover and explicitly state their needs as they go through these learning-by-doing cycles (Slaughter, 1993). They also have a high cost of exploring all aspects of a product and solution space (Franke & Schreier, 2002). Expert users, on the other hand, are usually professionals (such as designers) and they require a large solution space to design with direct access to all possible functions and options. Over time, a non-expert user may gain expertise, turn into an expert user, and require further freedom and sensitivity. Hence these users are not treated equally (Randall, Terwiesch, & Ulrich, 2005).

Non-expert Users: *A non-expert user does not already have specific solution information (and may not have need information in an explicit form) needed for innovation and design. The user needs to go through learning-by-doing cycles to develop a solution (and possibly need) information and has a high cost of going through these cycles.*

With the necessary definitions required to have a shared understanding of the key terms in the dissertation, the next and the final chapter of *Part I* outlines the structure of the dissertation.

4 Structure of the Dissertation

Toolkits, the central theme of the dissertation are artifacts, and as described in Chapter 2, they are the meeting point between the "*inner environment*" (the engineering substance and the structure of the artifact itself) and the "*outer environment*" (the surrounding it operates in) (Simon, 1969). The three studies of the dissertation aim to provide a balanced view of all three domains on the research question. The first study is in the domain of the "human" (or organization) with a focus on understanding how

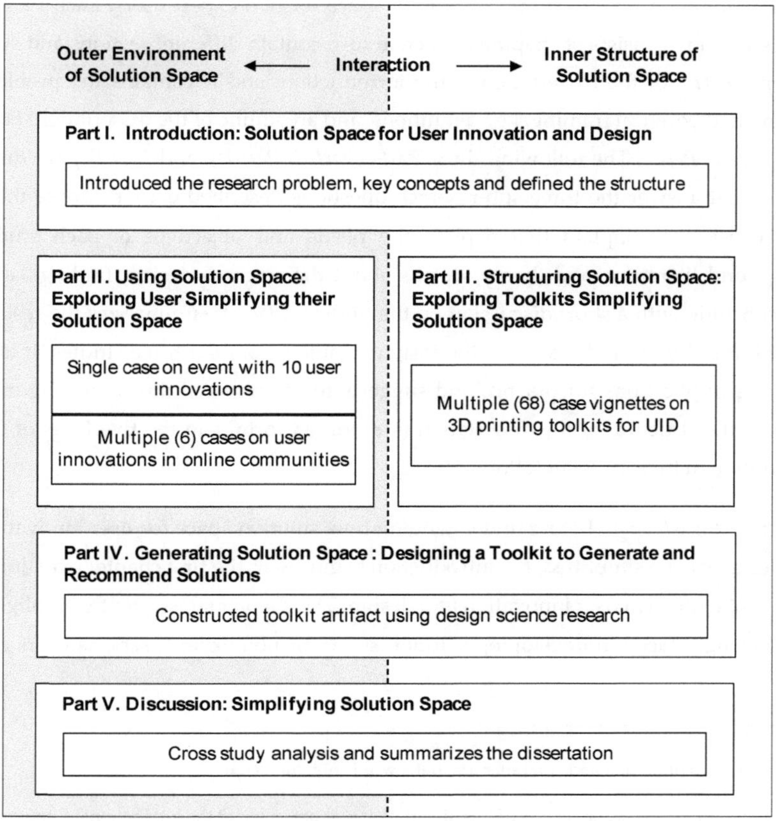

Figure 4: Overall Research Approach of the dissertation

users behave when they use toolkits in their settings. The second study is in the domain of the "computer" with a focus on the structure of the toolkit solution space[5]. The third study, on the other hand, follows design science research methodology and aims to develop design theories at the meeting point, where the previous two studies interact. This structure of the three studies closely follows from the focus and locus of design theory, initiated by Simon and extended by Chatterjee (Chatterjee, 2015; Simon, 1969) and can be seen in Figure 4.

The structure keeps the overall research approach of the dissertation in mind. The dissertation[6] contains five Parts, which altogether have the goal of improving the understanding on how to simplify solution space for non-expert users. Each Part of the dissertation consists of chapters, which in turn contain different sections and sub-sections. *Part I* of the dissertation is the introduction, and it contains the problem statement, theoretical framing, key definitions, and an outline of the dissertation. Four Parts follow *Part I*. The following three Parts (*Part II*, *Part III*, and *Part IV*) are three studies that answer the three sub-research questions described earlier[7]. These three Parts consist of chapters that explain the needs and objectives of each study, background literature, and theory, details about the research design, findings, and they conclude with a short discussion on the findings. *Part V* summarizes the results of the three studies and discusses the insights gained from the three studies. It also describes implications for practice and suggests future research directions. Figure 5 presents the structure of the dissertation in a unified form, and the five Parts of the dissertation in further detail follow.

Part I – Introduction: Before understanding how solution space for user innovation and design can be simplified, the introduction begins with the first chapter explaining the role of toolkits in user innovation and design. The chapter subsequently highlights the challenges faced in developing solution space for non-expert users, as users can

[5] The domain of human and computer are in the words of Simon (1969).

[6] A proposal for an earlier version of this dissertation was presented at the International Conference of Information Systems (ICIS) Doctoral Consortium in Milan (Naik, 2013).

[7] The research question and sub questions are in Chapter 1 of *Part I*.

potentially access increasingly large production capabilities. The next chapter sets a common understanding required for the rest of the dissertation by formally defining the key terms used, based on existing literature. The final chapter presents the structure of the dissertation along with the overall research process and explains the reasons behind them.

Part II – Using Solution Space: After the introduction, the next Part looks at the first sub-research question, which is asked in the human domain, i.e. from the user's perspective. It explores how users simplify solution space for innovation. Solution space for users who have access to different toolkits with different solution spaces can be much larger. The first chapter explains the needs and objectives of the study. The literature background required to understand the context of the study follows. The third chapter explains modularity theory which is the theoretical perspective used. The next chapter explains the research method used and the sample data. The study consists of two sub-studies: A single case study on a 12 days event for user innovation in the field of the Internet of Things (IoT) and a multiple case study on user innovations in online communities. These two sub-studies explore how users simplified their solution spaces while developing their innovative solutions. The next chapter presents the findings of these sub-studies. The sub-studies identified the process of developing user innovation artifacts and uncovered the use of 3D printing and low-cost computing to create *dynamic interfaces* that enable user innovation and design. The final chapter discusses these findings.

Part III – Structuring Solution Space: After exploring the users simplifying solution space, *Part III* explores toolkits simplifying solution space, effectively bringing the dissertation into the domain of the structure of toolkits. The first chapter explains the needs and objectives of the study and sets the research focus. The second chapter provides literature background that related to toolkit solution space. A chapter on the theoretical framework used to study toolkit solution space based on modularity theory follows it. The next chapter describes the research method and data used. The explorative study investigates contemporary toolkits in 3D printing using modularity-in-design and modularity-in-use as the theoretical lens. The next chapter presents the findings of the study. The study explores 68 case vignettes on 3D printing toolkits and develops a 2x2-matrix framework for categorizing toolkit solution space. This categorization and the relevant theory lead to four mechanisms used in toolkits to simplify solution space. The final chapter discusses these findings.

Part IV – Generating Solution Space: Having explored solution space from both the user and toolkit perspectives, *Part IV* looks at the interaction between these two domains and aims to answer its sub-research question by designing a toolkit. The first chapter describes the needs and objectives of the study as in the earlier Parts. The second chapter provides further literature specifically relevant to the research question and theory necessary for designing artifacts. The next chapter describes the design science research method used to design and its real world context. The study designed three artifacts, which together form a toolkit that generates and recommends solutions to users. The design of the toolkit exploits learnings from *Part II* and *Part III* and builds on established theory on recommender systems. The next chapter presents the findings of the study, which is in the form of a description of the artifacts and the evaluation of their design. The final chapter discusses these findings and connects them to previous studies.

Part V – Discussion: This is the final Part of the dissertation, and it summarizes the findings of the previous three Parts and discusses them. The research contributions and suggestions for practice follow next with a focus on cross-study analysis to bring out contributions to research and practice. Simplifying solution space to enable non-expert users in user innovation and design has implications for both user communities as well as product and toolkit firms. Future research directions and the conclusion mark the end of the dissertation.

Simplifying Solution Space:
Enabling Non-Expert Users to Innovate and Design with Toolkits

I. Introduction: Solution Space for User Innovation and Design

- Introduces solution space and the need to simplify it for non-expert users
- Introduces theoretical framing and defines toolkits for UID and solution space
- Outlines the structure of the thesis

II. Using Solution Space: Exploring Users Simplifying Solution Space

- Introduces modularity theory as a lens to study simplifying solution space
- Identifies the process of user innovation in making products
- Describes mechanisms followed by user innovators to simplify solution space

III. Structuring Solution Space: Exploring Toolkits Simplifying Solution Space

- Develops a framework based on modularity theory for categorizing solution space
- Identifies four mechanisms to simplify solution space in 3D printing toolkits
- Conceptualizes the design of 'meta-toolkits' for user-created toolkits

IV. Generating Solution Space: Designing a Toolkit to Generate and Recommend Solutions

- Outlines user innovation with implicit needs
- Outlines theory on recommender systems as a basis for this study
- Designs novel artifacts based on insights from Part II and Part III
- Evaluates the artifacts in experiments and workshops

V. Discussion: Simplifying Solution Space

- Summarizes and discusses findings from the three studies
- Discusses theoretical contributions and managerial recommendations for practice
- Provides future research directions and conclusion

Figure 5: Structure and Outcomes of the dissertation

Part II

Using Solution Space:

Exploring Users Simplifying Solution Space

1 Needs and Objectives

The first Part of the thesis introduced toolkits for UID and solution space and explained the challenge of simplifying a large solution space for non-expert users. *Part II*[8] of the thesis aims to answer how users simplify their solution space to innovate and design. A growing number of users can construct physical solutions that satisfy their special needs. Toolkits play a significant role in enabling these users to develop solution information (von Hippel & Katz, 2002), but it is important to understand the different steps of this development, the constraints users face, and the support they receive. Exploring how users manage the complexity of creating innovative solutions using multiple toolkits with many solution spaces leads to recommendations for simplifying solution space that enables non-expert users. Hence, this study aims to answer the first sub-research question:

RQ1: How do users simplify their solution space to create innovative solutions?

The motivation for this study stems from a lack of research on a user's solution space to innovate with multiple toolkits. Reiterating the first chapter on the challenge of simplifying solution space, both individual users and user firms innovate and develop new products that better solve their problems and fulfill their needs. However, transferring this need information to manufacturers or service providers can be very complex and time-consuming. Toolkits can enable users to perform need-related innovation tasks themselves. Toolkits have been studied as systems specific to a field, for example, integrated circuit design (von Hippel & Katz, 2002), or software game design (Prügl & Schreier, 2006) and are restricted to the solution space of the manufacturer's production system. An emerging trend in user innovation is working with multiple solution spaces from multiple toolkits. The user's perspective on innovation becomes even more complicated as technologies like 3D printing have

[8] An earlier version of this research has been presented at the Open and User Innovation Conference (OUI) 2014 as (Naik & Möslein, 2014)

toolkits for building components but not for complete products. This makes them necessary but not sufficient to create innovative products.

The context of 3D printing further explains the notion of users working with multiple solutions spaces. Despite 3D printing toolkits having a large solution space regarding the broad range of shapes they can design, they have some limitations (Snyder, 2014). Commercially used 3D printing technologies are mostly restricted to printing in a single material. Multi-material 3D printers in use are expensive, often proprietary, and limited to at most three materials (Sitthi-amorn, Lan, & Wang, 2015). Furthermore, the quality of 3D printing technologies varies drastically. Home printers do not always produce parts that meet necessary material characteristics (in terms of strength, reliability, etc.). Printing functional electronic components such as integrated circuits, motors, etc. is still a distant dream. Hence, users often need to assemble their products out of various components that could be either 3D printed or manufactured through other processes.

The objectives of the study are to explore user innovations from the users' perspective as they innovate and design with toolkits that possess multiple solution spaces and to identify how they simplify their solution space in this process. As a solution that meets user needs is the goal of the user innovation process, this study emphasizes user innovators and their associated solutions. The theoretical perspective of modularity as discussed in *Part I* is used as a lens to analyze the organization of the innovation process followed by users and firms and the evolution of the solution. Hence the relevant theoretical concepts here are modular organizations (Sanchez & Mahoney, 1996; Schilling, 2000), as well as modularity-in-design and modularity-in-production (Baldwin & Clark, 2004).

The explorative study follows a case study research approach using the above theoretical perspective (Yin, 2009). The empirical context for the study is user innovations in products involving technologies such as 3D printing and open hardware electronics (as seen *in "maker communities"* and closely related *"maker events"*[9]). The users innovate and develop products that belong to various industry

[9] Chapter 2 further discusses maker communities and maker events.

domains. The study describes user innovations themselves, the characteristics of systems used to design them, and the use of the solution space, and identifies models for simplification of solution space.

This study forms *Part II* of the thesis and consists of five chapters. Following the introduction in chapter 1, chapter 2 and chapter 3 present the literature background and theoretical underpinning of the study. Chapter 4 describes the selected research design, details the processes of data gathering and analysis, and presents the empirical data under study. Chapter 5 presents the main findings of the study. The final chapter 6 consists of discussions on this study and areas of future research.

2 Understanding the Context

This chapter describes briefly the necessary literature background needed before going into further details of the study. As the objectives of the study are to explore how users simplify their solution space when creating innovative solutions, it begins with some primary background literature on user innovation, the importance of lead users and communities, and the role of sticky information. This section leads to literature on toolkits and their solution spaces. As the empirical context of the study is user innovation in making tangible products, the next section describes the latest research on users making products using technologies such as 3D printing and open hardware electronics in communities and events. The literature background sets the stage for the next chapter that discusses the research method and data.

2.1 User Innovation

Von Hippel conceptualized the term user innovation along with identifying the customer-active paradigm, where the customer actively develops an innovative product idea and takes it to the manufacturer (von Hippel, 1978a). He looked at the industry of scientific instruments and found that users dominated the number of innovations instead of manufacturers, by inventing, prototyping and field testing innovations (von Hippel, 1976). A study on the semiconductor and electronic sub-assembly industry once again reported the significant share of innovations from users and user firms using the equipment rather than the equipment manufacturer (von Hippel, 1977). However, the role of users in the innovation process has been observed even earlier, with cases documented from the 1960s showing significant user contributions (Bogers, Afuah, & Bastian, 2010).

2.1.1 User Firms as Innovators

Both individual end users and user firms develop new products and processes in various industries. User firms are credited to innovations in diverse industries such as oil refining (Enos, 1962), chemical industry (Freeman et al., 1968), innovative industrial processes (Foxall & Tierney, 1984), construction industry (Slaughter, 1993),

Table 1: Compilation (non-exhaustive) of instances of innovation by user firms

Industry	**Instances of Innovation by User Firms**
Banking Services	55% of computerized commercial banking services were first developed and implemented by non-bank firms for their use (Oliveira & von Hippel, 2011)
Industrial Robotics	Firms that are both users and producers offer more advanced features (Roy, 2009)
Oil refining	Refining firms, users of the technology developed improvements and new processes (Enos, 1962)
Chemicals	Major process innovations came from chemical companies running process plants (Freeman et al., 1968)
Scientific instruments	80% of the innovations that offered a significant increment in utility were invented, prototyped and field tested by users (von Hippel, 1976)
Semiconductors and electronics	Process machinery user rather than the manufacturer dominates the innovation process (von Hippel, 1977)
Clinical equipment	Medical equipment used to determine levels of chemical constituents of blood developed and used by laboratory clinicians (von Hippel & Finkelstein, 1979)
Aerospace	Tools used in the aerospace industry were initiated and developed by the aerospace firm (Foxall & Tierney, 1984)
Applications Software	User presence in all stages of innovation: need recognition, idea formulation, development and commercialization (Voss, 1985) User firms of Apache web server software modified the software to better meet their specific needs (Franke & von Hippel, 2003)
Residential construction	User-builders were exclusive source of innovations that involved integration of components from suppliers (Slaughter, 1991)
Automobiles	Japanese suppliers of machine tool for cars got investments, direct development inputs by Japanese car producers (Lee, 1996)
Electronics	Japanese electronics firms developed computer controlled tools for their production (Lee, 1996)
Convenience stores	Innovation in store inventory management in convenience stores was initiated by the store (Ogawa, 1998)

development of machine tools (Lee, 1996), convenience stores (Ogawa, 1998) and in the software industry (Voss, 1985). Table 1 compiles a non-exhaustive list of instances of user innovations seen in firms, to highlight the industrial diversity of this phenomenon. User innovation among end users is also very diverse as the next section demonstrates.

2.1.2 End Users as Innovators

Users as a valuable source of ideas, and methods to identify them have been discussed in marketing research (von Hippel, 1978b), von Hippel went further and identified "lead users" to a product or process who have strong needs that can become general market needs in the future. They often attempt to meet their unfulfilled needs by designing and developing new products and processes and, thus, can provide new concept and design ideas as well as user need-forecasting (von Hippel, 1986). Lead users are seen influencing the development of information systems as in the library users of OPAC information search systems (Morrison, Roberts, & von Hippel, 2000,) and security software developed by users (Franke & von Hippel, 2003). The lead user concept was further explained along with mechanisms of identifying them with studies in various industries such as computer-aided systems for the design of printed circuit boards (Urban & von Hippel, 1988), construction products and materials (Herstatt & von Hippel, 1992) and in developing innovative services in banking (Oliveira & von Hippel, 2011; von Hippel & Riggs, 1996).

User innovation from end users is also present in user communities especially in products used by hobbyists and enthusiasts (von Hippel, 2005). Users freely reveal their innovations, so they benefit as a whole without having to independently innovate by themselves (Harhoff, Henkel, & von Hippel, 2003). The open source software movement demonstrates typical examples for user innovation communities. Development of open source software has distributed management and has significant contributions from end users. The Linux operating system and Apache server software are well-known examples of open source software that were developed by programmer-users of these software (Harhoff et al., 2003; Lakhani & Von Hippel, 2003). Open source communities are usually not firm hosted and can spawn around open source projects in software as well as hardware (Balka, Raasch, & Herstatt, 2009;

Raasch, Herstatt, & Balka, 2009). These communities can also consist of professional users as seen in Salesforce.com's IdeaExchange or a mix of corporate and individual end users as in Dell IdeaStorm (Li, Kankanhalli, & Kim, 2016). Selective openness by firms in consumer electronics and information technology hardware industries has been shown to have an impact on user involvement and contributions in firm driven user innovation communities (Balka, Raasch, & Herstatt, 2014).

User innovation communities are not limited to software and electronics. Studies have shown that user innovation communities provide value to developing physical products in the field of sporting equipment used in the extreme sports of canyoning, sailplaning, boardercross and cycling (Franke & Shah, 2003). Similar instances of user innovation communities were found in sporting goods and mountain-biking (Baldwin, Hienerth, & von Hippel, 2006; Lüthje, 2004; Lüthje, Herstatt, & von Hippel, 2005; Raasch, Herstatt, & Lock, 2008; Tietz, R., Morrison, P. D., Luthje, C., & Herstatt, 2005).

Communities of lead users bring additional value when compared to regular user innovation communities as their contributions stem from their ability to develop solution information instead of simply describing problems or stating customer needs (Mahr & Lievens, 2012). The capability of an innovation community to go beyond just ideation to implementation is critical to creating business value. That is, the capability to select user-generated ideas from the community for innovation development and then introduce the developed innovation to the desired users via the community (Dong & Wu, 2015).

2.1.3 Sticky Information

While users are a valuable source for innovations and lead users can identify upcoming innovations, there can be problems with shifting this need information from the user to the manufacturer when the information is "sticky." Stickiness is the incremental expenditure required in transferring the information from one place to another in a form that is accessible by the information seeker. This problem limits the realization of innovations based on user needs. Stickiness can depend on the type of information, the information provider or seeker, or the mode of interaction in between them (von Hippel, 1994). The concept of information stickiness is similar to tacit knowledge (Brodbeck & Polanyi, 1960). This inherent stickiness of information has been observed in the user innovation communities in sporting equipment mentioned above (Franke & Shah, 2003). Because of this nature of sticky information, many users are not aware of their needs and are not able to formulate these needs explicitly. However, users who engage in learning-by-doing processes can develop new products (Slaughter, 1993), thus suggesting the use of toolkits for user innovation as a means of solving the problem of sticky information. The next section further explains this concept.

2.2 Toolkits for User Innovation

Toolkits, as defined by von Hippel and Katz, refer to systems offered to users to innovate through a learning-by-doing process. Toolkits give their users some of the design capability of the firm and thus do the job of transferring the manufacturer's solution information to user-innovators, thereby reducing the stickiness of problem-related knowledge mentioned in the previous section. Integrating user innovation and design ideas requires a connection between problem information found among users and the solution information usually found in firms. The interaction and information cost arising in this process can be handled by information systems which guide users, either through a basic configuration process or even enable them to develop innovative solutions resulting from their specific needs (von Hippel, 2001; von Hippel & Katz, 2002).

Solution space is one of the five main characteristics of toolkits for user innovation as described earlier in *Part I*. Toolkits offer users a 'solution space' of design freedom not exceeding the manufacturer's production capabilities. Users learn to innovate and design solutions by performing learning cycles of trial-and-error in the solution space. Well-designed toolkits are user-friendly enough so users can learn without additional training. Toolkits contain libraries of standard modules or presets that can act as a starting point for users' design changes. Also, properly designed toolkits ensure that the solution space of toolkits is such that the manufacturer can produce user-designed products or services without requiring any further revisions (von Hippel & Katz, 2002). Prügl and Schreier (2006) classify toolkits into expert and basic toolkits based on the solution space they offer to users. The remainder of this section discusses expert toolkits as they deal with user innovation rather than customization, which is relevant for the study. *Part III* discusses basic toolkits further.

Expert toolkits (or high-end toolkits) for user innovation are described as a source of radical innovations, which offer theoretically unlimited solution space to the users within the manufacturer's production capabilities (Franke & Schreier, 2002). Thus, they create radical solutions to both existing and new problems, generate new functions, and even create entirely new products. They tend to be more challenging to use and demand greater user skill and so are appropriate for expert users (Prügl & Schreier, 2006). Lead users who have significantly altered a product or developed new product functionalities for their personal or in-house use can use expert toolkits when there are not satisfied by standard products. Firms have used expert toolkits to "plant" and "grow" innovators among their user base. Lead users using toolkits have been known to develop modules which, if proven to be popular and error free, get later incorporated into the standard versions of the products. This incorporation is seen as in the cases of the statistical analysis software firm Stata and toolkits for the computer game The Sims (Franke & Schreier, 2002; Prügl & Schreier, 2006).

The study on toolkits used in The Sims gives further valuable insights on the usage of toolkits by lead users. Lead-user innovators consider their innovation engagements a long lasting experience that is continuous, evolving, and intense. They are sometimes not content with the official toolkits provided by the manufacturer and resort to using their own toolkits to push further their design possibilities. Furthermore, user created designs and user created toolkits are sometimes not just own creations used only by their creators, but have a high demand among other users as well. It suggests that firms can incorporate user created toolkits along with user created designs into their standard offerings.

Toolkits have also equipped lead users in the form of individuals or groups of individuals to contribute to product design without having all the necessary skills to design a product from scratch. Toolkits achieve this by providing libraries that give users similar capabilities by letting them convert their innovative ideas into novel solutions by combining different modules and not having to work from scratch (von

Hippel & Katz, 2002). Furthermore, user communities often accompany expert toolkits, which assist in problem-solving and diffusion of toolkit related information (L. Jeppesen, 2003). A properly designed toolkit which encourages learning-by-doing and has an active community can train non-expert users to increase their expertise as in the Sims (Prügl & Schreier, 2006). In the context of making tangible products, toolkits can be either software, hardware, or both. The next section further explains toolkits in the context of this study.

2.3 Solution Space for Making

This study has a context of user innovation with new production technologies like 3D printing and focusses on the emerging phenomenon of 'making' tangible products. Users making physical product innovations has been driven by technologies like 3D printing and open hardware (Balka et al., 2009) such as Arduino microcontrollers, which have introduced innovation opportunities by faster prototyping and easier availability of parts through direct online distribution. Social interconnectedness due to growing participation of people from different communities, skills, and interests have played a significant role as well (Honey & Kanter, 2013). Maker events extend the approach of online open design communities by offering a localized social gathering for a fixed time that accelerates knowledge sharing among the community members (Chorianopoulos, Jaccheri, & Nossum, 2012).

A consumer 3D printer accompanied with 3D design software provides users design feedback cycles that allow them to design innovative products with a learning-by-doing process. Consumer 3D printers typically print in various plastics. They are computer-controlled machines that successively lay out layers of material to create the desired shape of the object. It follows an additive process, which contrasts with traditional subtractive processes of machining, where the material is removed using methods such as cutting and drilling. An increasing number of online 3D printing services and marketplaces supplement consumer printers as means for users to print their designs. As this technology can print in virtually any shape and a diverse set of materials that include metal and ceramic (Anderson & Sherman, 2007; Snyder, 2014) it provides users with a large solution space.

Using these technologies, users have been developing and sharing 3D designs in online user communities. The online community Thingiverse, which was started by 3D printer manufacturer Makerbot is known as an online community where designs have extensively branched out because of its open source network nature (Kyriakou, Englehardt, & Nickerson, 2012; West & Kuk, 2014).

In the offline world, the idea of a dedicated location to make tangible objects, a "makerspace" has taken hold where users can get together, learn and develop through complex design and making practices (Sheridan et al., 2014). These makerspaces contain equipment for rapid prototyping and digital fabrication. Events called "hackathons" which were initially conducted for developing new software, now are carried out in these makerspaces using these technologies and they include "maker events" that allow rapid prototyping and development (Briscoe & Mulligan, 2014; Sydow, 2015).

With this necessary context for the study, the next chapter delves into the theory for conducting the study. Users as they innovate and design in these communities and events employ principles of modularity theory. The next chapter summarizes aspects of modularity that forms the theoretical lens for conducting this study.

3 Theoretical Underpinning

Theory on modularity as described in *Part I* is a useful viewpoint to understand both organizational forms as well as product design. It is a general systems concept that describes the degree to which components can be separated and recombined. This refers to the rules of the system architecture which enable or prohibit the mixing and matching of components (Schilling, 2000). The theory is especially suited for this study because modularity is distributed nature enables simplification. As this study explores how user innovators simplify their solution space, the focus is on exploring and identifying how solution space is simplified through occurrences of modularity, as users organize their innovation activities with others, and as they develop their innovative solutions.

Modularity in organizations marks a shift from large hierarchical integrated organizations that have disaggregated into loosely coupled organizations that work together with coupled production arrangements. Through this change, firms can specialize in their respective competencies while offering more heterogeneous products and services. Heterogeneity in inputs and demands drives interfirm modularity and competition acts as a catalyst (Schilling, 2000). In the context of user innovation, organizational modularity is in between users themselves and between users and firms. They work together to establish modularity-in-design and share the design load between them (Baldwin & Clark, 2004). Organizing can range between increasing modularity and growing integration depending strategic goals as is explained in Table 2.

Modularity in products makes it easier for lead users to develop focused product functions without having to redesign the whole product. Users can also develop complex products traditionally developed by large teams using pre-designed customizable modules, which would have required much more labor when designed from scratch even by experienced users (Baldwin & Clark, 2004).

An example for such a case of a modular toolkit is the open source Drupal Content Management System. It consists of various modules developed by its open source community, each of which users can easily configure. Every user can then develop a distinct platform using a unique combination of Drupal's modules configured to the user's needs. Lead users with sufficient PHP programming knowledge can develop their innovative modules and offer it to other users in the Drupal community. Thus, the Drupal website hosts and offers to other users established modules developed in a distributed fashion. Hence, it exhibits modularity-in-design, modularity-in-production as well as modularity-in-use (Baldwin & Clark, 2001, 2004).

Table 2: Factors driving modularity and integration, based on Schilling (2000)

Driving Modularity	**Driving Integration**
Heterogeneity of customer needs	Increasing market power
Heterogeneity of components needed	Maintaining architectural control
Environmental pressures from • Competition • Technology change • Creation of standards	Specificity in components

3.1 Operations in Modularity

Baldwin and Clark summarize six core design operators of a modular system (Baldwin & Clark, 2001). These operators are relevant in both the context of organizations and product design. In product system design, these operators apply in a more top-down fashion while they evolve bottom-up in organizations. These operators provide flexibility in design as long as new design follows the underlying design rules. The basic operators are the following: 1) Splitting into independent modules, 2) Substituting of modules in a system, 3) Excluding modules to modify the system, 4) Augmenting new modules into the system, 5) Inverting the order of module dependencies, and 6) Porting modules to use in different contexts. These operators have led to other derivations such as linking, recombining, and extending modules, which

Table 3 describes along with the basic six operations.

Table 3: Operations on modular systems based on Baldwin and Clark (2004)

Operations	Description
Splitting	A combination of different modules can replace a module. It increases the options in the system and can increase economic value
Substituting	A module can be replaced by another improved module as long as the design rules are followed in the new module
Excluding	A module of the system can be excluded if the value it brings in is not needed or introduces new problems
Augmenting	A new module can be introduced to the system that provides additional value to the system
Inverting	The hierarchy of modules can be changed by creating a new grouping of design rules that is separated from the architectural module
Porting	A module can be ported to another system by creating a "shell" so that it works for systems other than that for which it was designed
Linking	Pre-existing modules can be linked differently to create new functionalities
Recombining	Linked modules can be integrated to create efficiencies at the cost of losing the option generated. It is the opposite of the splitting operator
Extending	Modules can be extended by modifying them to provide additional value

3.2 Interfaces in Modularity

Modular systems connect to each other, and with their connection, they interact with each other and exchange resources or data (Sahaym, Steensma, & Schilling, 2007). Modular interfaces in products can be of two types. Firstly, they can be three dimensional as in the case of physical interfaces between two mechanical objects. Secondly, they can be one or two-dimensional, as in computer systems where these interfaces then could be informational or used to transmit electrical power (Whitney, 2004). Table 4 explains these types of interfaces using examples.

Table 4: Types of interfaces in modular product systems

Types of Interfaces	Examples
Physical Interfaces	Plugs and sockets so that two modules that follow standards in dimensions so that they can physically fit together (Whitney, 2004)
Information Interfaces	Two modules that follow the same communication protocol, so they can transfer information to each other (Whitney, 2004)
Resource Interfaces	Power wiring through plugs and sockets to transfer electrical power between the modules (Sahaym et al., 2007)

Modularity in design has well-known benefits such as cost reduction, lesser learning time, design flexibility, and customization. It certainly has impacted the computer industry both regarding software and hardware (Baldwin & Clark, 2001, 2004). Open source hardware platforms using modular electronics like the Arduino along with open source 3D designs are poised to impact specialized equipment manufacturing as well (Pearce, 2012).

4 Method and Data

This chapter presents the method and data used to identify how users simplify solution space when creating innovative products. The chapter divides into three sections. The first section places the research approach followed in *Part II* within the overall research approach of the thesis. The second section describes the research design in detail which includes the method used, data collection processes followed, and data analysis in the two sub-studies. The third section describes the empirical data samples, which consists of cases of user innovations.

4.1 Research Approach

The objective of this Part is to study how users simplify their solution space when creating innovative solutions. The context for this study is user innovation in creating tangible products, where users innovate using new digital fabrication technologies like 3D printing, electronics, and related software. As this is rather a new phenomenon, explorative qualitative research approach is appropriate for its study. The case study research method is, particularly suited for this study as it can investigate a contemporary phenomenon in depth and within its real-life context, especially when the boundaries between phenomenon and context are not evident. Case study research is preferred to address "How" or "Why" questions that deal with contemporary events where no control of behavioral events is required. Furthermore, it relies on multiple sources of evidence such as documents, archival records, interviews, direct observation, participant observation, and physical artifacts that were available for this study (Yin, 2009).

The overall study in this Part is consists of *two sub-studies* that follow case study research methods to gather data and analyze two aspects of this phenomenon. The first sub-study gives an in depth concurrent look at users early in the design process, while second sub-study gives an in-depth look at the users who have designed established user innovations. The first case study is a single case study on an event users made innovative IoT products, comprising of 40 users divided into groups developing innovative products over a period of around two weeks. It gives a close look at user innovation in this context by direct access to the participants and observing the design process over its duration. The second sub-study consists of six

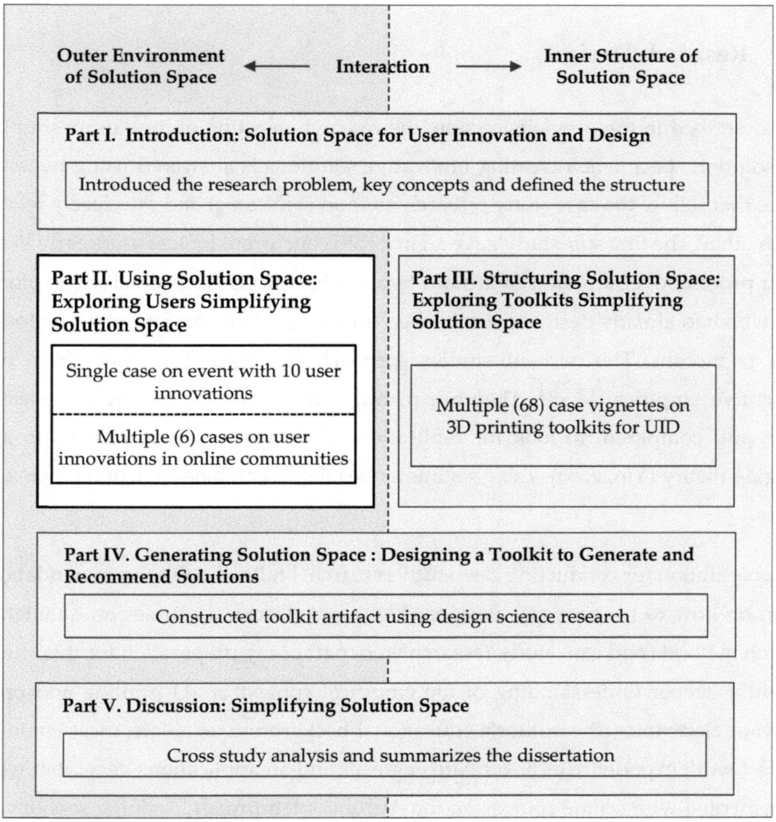

Figure 6: Part II within the overall dissertation research approach

multiple cases on user innovations chosen from online open source communities related to 3D Printing. This sub-study gives an in-depth understanding of how users had designed established products over a longer period. Together, the two sub-studies aim to draw accurate and reliable conclusions from data, both from the early stages as well as later stages or after the development process.

The research approach of this study follows the overall research approach and structure of the dissertation. Figure 6 presents the research approach of *Part II* in the overall context of the dissertation. The research design section explains in further detail the selection of cases, case details and data analysis for the study.

4.2 Research Design

As described in the previous section, the research question of how users simplify their solution space when creating innovative solutions is answered using two sub-studies that follow the case study research method (Yin, 2009) and are closely related to each other. The first sub-study gave an in depth concurrent look at users early in the design process, over a period of around two weeks. The second sub-study explored users who had already designed established user innovations over a longer period of six to 12 months. The two sub-studies approach the research problem from two consecutive empirical levels. They are placed side-by-side in the overall research design and compared, to look for replications, differences, and extensions to any emerging theory (Yin, 2009). Table 5 summarizes the research designs of the two sub-studies.

In preparation for conducting case study research, I followed the recommendations by Yin on how to prepare case designs (Yin, 2009). Doctoral courses on qualitative research methods and case study research were part of my preparation for this study. To gain a deeper understanding of the empirical context of 3D printing and open hardware electronics, the author's educational background as an electrical engineer and past work experience as a software engineer and an applications developer were supplemented with online courses on the Arduino platform and training sessions on digital fabrication techniques. The next step was the development of a case study protocol that guided the data collection process, based on the recommendations of Yin.

It was followed by screening candidate cases to select cases that yielded the best data and were sufficient in number following a replication design (Yin, 2009).

Table 5: Summarized research designs of the two sub-studies in Part II

Research Design Details	Sub-Study 1	Sub-Study 2
Research Question	How do users simplify their solution space to create innovative solutions?	
Unit of Analysis	Solution space of users Solution space of user team	Solution space of users
Design Type Selection	Single Case Study	Multiple Case Study
Case Study Protocol	Developed based on recommendations from Yin (2009)	
Case Sample	Event with 40 users designing 10 innovative products	Six existing innovations by users in an online community
Theory	Modularity in organization and design	
Data Sources	Semi-structured interviews, surveys, direct observations, physical artifacts, presentations and reports	Semi-structured interviews, documentation, release histories, community discussions, websites, and other published material
Data Collection Principles used	Multiple sources of evidence, case study database, replication, pattern matching	
Data Analysis Techniques	Coding based on theory and empirical codes within case	Coding based on theory and empirical codes within and cross-case-analysis cases
Analysis Strategy	Identify characteristics of toolkits and solution space used Identify the process followed by users Draw conclusions	

In both sub-studies, users work with multiple toolkits and multiple solution spaces each restricted to a specific application area. As this Part addresses simplification of the overall solution space for the user, the two sub-studies emphasize on the following. Firstly, the characteristics of toolkits and solution space used to develop their innovations and secondly, the process followed by users for developing their innovations is studied. The following sections describe the research design followed for each of the two sub-studies in further detail.

4.2.1 Research Design for Sub-study 1

The first case study follows a single case design on an event for making innovative IoT products that lasted for around two weeks with 40 participants. The participants divided themselves into teams, which worked together as they developed innovative products using 3D printing, and open source electronics that aimed to solve real world problems. As they were under observation for the duration of the event, it provided valuable data on the process users followed when innovating and designing tangible products. Furthermore, the participants worked together in teams on their innovative products, providing empirical evidence on user innovation done in teams. Hence, the case has two units of analysis. The first unit of analysis is the solution space of each user and the second unit of analysis is the solution space of the team working together.

4.2.1.1 Case Sampling

A single case design on only one such event was chosen as it was a critical case on the upcoming phenomena of maker events or hackathons, which have had limited social science inquiry. The sub-study selected the event IoT Start-up Summer School[10] for the in-depth case as the event program followed the approach user innovators take to build new products. It follows a similar format to other maker events conducted in the past that promoted user innovation in digital fabrication, such as "Think.Make.Start"[11]. The case also met the relevant context of the study as participants used 3D printing and electronics toolkits to build innovative products. Furthermore, this particular event was chosen as a case as it had a high likelihood to yield the best data due to the researcher's access to directly observe the event as one of the organizers (Yin, 2009).

---

[10] IoT Start-up Summer School was organized by Friedrich Alexander University Erlangen-Nürnberg and UnternehmerTUM in Munich as part of STARTIFY7, a European Union funded project to promote entrepreneurship in ICT technologies.

[11] Think.Make.Start is a recurring prototyping workshop for 14 days where participants can develop and build innovative products with inputs from experts from industry and research. It is conducted by UnternehmerTUM in their high-tech prototyping area called MakerSpace.

The academy targeted young candidates from maker and startup communities, to encourage them to design products around identifiable needs and plan business models around their products. The participants were young adults between the ages 18 and 29, with a gender distribution of 13 females to 27 males. Thirteen of the participants had a business background, 17 with a technology background and ten with a combination of both. The academy selected the participants out of a larger pool of over 200 applicants based on their background in the field of IoT and motivation to develop market ready innovative products in this area.

4.2.1.2 Data Collection and Analysis

Data collection for this study was primarily through multiple sources and guided by the research question and the theoretical perspective of modular organizations, design, operations, and interfaces discussed in the previous chapter. Data collection occurred through five sources. Firstly, the ten teams were each interviewed three times during the period. The average total interview time spent with a team was 101.5 min (all three interviews). The interviews were semi-structured and conducted through open-ended questions to so that the participants could freely articulate their answers[12]. Secondly, the participants individually filled in two surveys during the event[13]. Thirdly, the progress of the products they developed was tracked, and toolkits used in designing their products were recorded. Fourthly, the teams pitched their business ideas along with demonstrations of their working prototypes twice during the event. Fifthly, the teams also submitted a short report on their planned business idea and description of their prototype, which the analysis also uses. All the data was collected in a case database consisting of notes, case study documents, tabular materials, and narratives in line with the case protocol.

These multiple data sources provide in-depth data to explore the issue at hand and lead to the triangulation of data sources that improves the case studies. Furthermore, data points taken from different points of time in these two weeks mean that the entire

[12] The questionnaire for the interviews is in Annex A.

[13] The survey questionnaire is in Annex C.

process of prototyping was tracked with longitudinal observations for the period of the event (Yin, 2009). Data analysis was done by following an explanation building approach by analyzing data and establishing "how" users simplified their solution space and iteratively revising the emerging patterns or propositions. As the event was well documented for the period of two weeks, a time series analysis was also conducted to find any observable empirical trends that seem to replicate among the users and user teams in the case study. The theoretical underpinning of modularity formed the basis for apriori codes for examining the data. However, empirical codes were also generated when available, following the constant comparative method (Glaser, 1965). It gave the possibility of generating new theory (Eisenhardt, 1989), within the limits of the theoretical perspective of modularity theory.

4.2.2 Research Design for Sub-study 2

The second sub-study follows a multiple case design on user innovations and consists of six cases. These cases are on innovations by users who used 3D printing technologies with the solution space of the users to design their products as the units of analysis. Using the case study research method on innovative users and the products they designed brings out the user side of user innovation. More importantly, it focuses on the usage of toolkits and other systems over a period, leading to the development of the products. Sub-study 2 follows a multiple case design as it allows cross-case analysis between cases thus integrating different and potentially alternative viewpoints of various users for the phenomena. They also typically build a stronger base for theory building (Yin, 2009).

4.2.2.1 Case Sampling

Selection of an appropriate sample of relevant cases is critical to ensure that the research study is in-depth and can lead to replication of findings or contrary findings. The goal of case sampling here was to select a sample of users with innovations in the field of 3D printing that are substantially significant instances and to find other cases that replicate or extend any emergent theory. Yin recommends the replication design for greater generalizability of findings (Yin, 2009). Guidelines for theoretical sampling from Eisenhardt also emphasize replication, and they helped to reduce selection bias as much as possible while extracting generalizable implications from the findings (Eisenhardt, 1989).

The study was limited to open source user innovations, i.e. products whose designs are open source. Open source products have rich data available in the form of design source, code, documentation, and discussion communities that can be better utilized using a case study approach. To build the sample of open source user innovations connected to 3D printing, popular online maker communities that work with 3D printing were investigated. These were (1) Thingiverse a leading 3D design community for discovering, making, and sharing 3D printable things that also has designs for electronic gadgets and (2) Instructables the maker community.

User innovations in these communities differed between those that had electronic components and those having only mechanical components, so they were treated separately. Two cases were chosen that represent these two groups of user innovations and were significant innovations, i.e., they were innovative solutions that required considerable time and resources to design, aimed at user needs and were better than other similar offerings in the market. They also had a growing influence in their communities, had received inputs from community members, and others often replicated their solutions. The first case of *Robohand* was purely mechanical, but vital as it brought down the cost of developing a customized prosthetic hand, by a factor of a few hundred times to almost only the cost of only the raw materials. The second case of *Koruza* extensively used standard electronics and 3D printed parts once again, to bring down the cost of laser wireless internet device significantly.

These two cases were extended by four supplementary cases to bring in more variety in the different pathways taken by the users in developing their innovations and in exploring replicability of the findings. They were selected following the same sampling process and hence, two of the supplementary cases are purely mechanical while two also include electronic components. Including additional cases reduces bias from individual sources of data and follows the recommendation of Eisenhardt that the optimal case number for building theory is between four and ten cases (Eisenhardt, 1991).

One main case study and two supplementary case studies with electronic components used the Arduino microcontroller and platform (however, Koruza later replaced the Arduino with the Raspberry Pi). The selection is based on a basic exploratory overview study on different hardware based platforms offered to end users. From a variety of modular electronics platforms that allow user innovations along with the Arduino such as *Lego Mindstorms, Littlebits, Ninja Blocks, Raspberry Pi, Tessel,* and *Twine*[14] it was seen that users who created innovative products worked with open platforms like Arduino often, where the openness provides design flexibility.

4.2.2.2 Data Collection and Analysis

This multiple case study on user innovations had multiple sources of data such as user innovator interviews, their web pages, published articles on the user innovations, and the innovation artifact itself. The multiple sources of evidence add richness to the cases, enable in-depth analysis and give the possibility of data source triangulation (Yin, 2009). Data on the artifact was collected from the design of the artifact, related documentation, and artifact demonstrations. The design history of the user innovations and associated discussions also allow us to investigate causes and relationships in detail and over a period (Runeson & Höst, 2008).

Although the user innovators were part of online communities, they submitted their creations individually. Therefore, individual users were interviewed. The interviews with the user innovators lasted between 30 to 60 minutes. The case on Robohand includes interviews of the user innovator, Richard and another key member of the community with major contributions. The case on Koruza used interviews conducted in 2013 and 2015 along with communication on updates in between, thus giving a longitudinal dimension to the data collected. The interviews have been carried out with the help of an interview guideline for semi-structured interviews consisting of open questions[15]. This approach was deliberately chosen so that the interviewees could freely express their opinions and full experiences. On receiving explicit consent from

[14] Please have a look at the glossary in Annex E for more information on these terms.

[15] The interview questionnaire can be found in Annex A

the interviewee, the interview was recorded, transcribed, and commented before analysis. Else, key points of the interview were noted down and augmented with other data sources mentioned above. In some of the cases, the user innovators answered open-ended questions over email because they preferred the flexibility to respond to questions asynchronously. Data from the documentation, release histories, community discussions, websites, online videos, and other published material were downloaded and saved in a local database. This data along with the data from the interviews was coded based on apriori concepts from modularity theory and characteristics of toolkits for user innovation described earlier. Emergent codes were also documented to identify important sub-categories or unforeseen concepts (Yin, 2009). Analysis for emergent codes was done following the constant comparative method (Glaser, 1965), where every coded data point was noted and compared against other incidents for similarities and differences and labeled as such and grouped. It established a classification of product characteristics in terms of interfaces and operations allowed as well as how user innovators used solution space to develop their novel products. The classification system was developed based on combined inputs from discussions with two independent researchers. Eventually, the analysis led to a model on how users simplified solution space when designing innovative solutions.

4.3 Case details

Following the research design of the two sub-studies in the previous section, the section further describes the details of the cases used in the two sub-studies. The first sub-study explores how users simplify solution space early in the design process, in the event that took place over a period of around two weeks. The second sub-study explored how users who had already designed established user innovations over a longer period of six to 12 months simplified their solution space.

4.3.1 Case Details for Sub-study 1

The first sub-study is a single case study on an event themed on Internet of Things, for training and promoting participants to design and develop innovative products based on user needs that can in the future be part of market-ready products or services. The interactive academy provided participants workshop tools, open source electronic hardware and end user 3D printing technologies, which were similar to the tools and technologies used by open source maker communities.

Program: The program structure had a strong emphasis on teamwork, hands-on learning, and workshops. The participants spent the first two days of the event familiarizing themselves by attending presentations and interactive workshops with the fields of IoT, design thinking, ideation, user needs, and prototyping. Day 3 onwards the participants formed teams and started prototyping their products. The time spent on prototyping versus attending training sections increased from Day 4 onwards, with more than 85% of the time dedicated to prototyping. The participants also carried their prototyping equipment and work on their products even after working hours. While the participants were mostly independent in how they designed their products and developed their market needs, they received regular feedback from trainers and workshop mentors. Trainers were present for an average of two hours out of which they conducted presentations for 60-90 minutes and used the rest of the time for discussions. At any point of time, 2-4 mentors accompanied the participants and gave them preliminary evaluations of their ideas.

Team formation: Interactive workshops on ideation conducted in the first two and a half days with exercises for groups drawn on random. These group exercises allowed the participants to familiarize themselves and have the first set of ideas, which they can further develop. On the third day, they self-organized into teams and start building their products. The participants organized themselves and worked in 10 teams of 3-5 members. They sought to form mixed teams of technical and non-technical participants. Three of the ten teams consisted of all participants with a technical background, while one team comprised of all non-technical participants.

User Needs: The participants identified user needs based on their experiences and designed innovative Internet of Things products to solve these needs. They further verified these user needs by evaluating their products with potential users.

Design Process: After that, they organized themselves into teams and started brainstorming and evaluating potential ideas as well as prototyping them. The participants worked within their teams, continuously designing and evaluating their prototypes. They also received regular technology tutorials on open source electronics like the Arduino, Raspberry Pi, etc., software related to the field (such as *Thingworx*[16]), and business tutorials such as business modeling and funding. The participants had full control on the tools they chose and design decisions of the prototyping process. Also, they also had the opportunity to get help from experienced mentors during the prototyping sessions. Furthermore, they also had the facility to use a 3D printer and a laser cutter if required. The evaluation of their ideas and prototypes happened at multiple levels. The teams regularly pitched their ideas to potential investors and industry experts, who gave them valuable feedback on what the market required. Furthermore, the teams also interacted heavily with potential customers and industry experts outside the event, by engaging in face-to-face interviews, phone calls and conducting surveys. Hence, they followed a rigorous cycle of design and evaluation during the period to develop an innovative product that has a legitimate market need.

Innovative Products Created: Table 6 summarizes Key details about the ten user teams and their innovative products. The teams designed these products for a variety of uses, from add-ons to action cameras to marketing campaigns using drones. The design ideas came from team members who identified these needs for themselves and evaluated these needs by talking to other potential users.

[16] Thingworx offers IoT software platforms.

Table 6: Products developed by maker teams and their need evaluations

Team Name	Artifact	Team Size	Customer Target	Need Evaluations
SensePro	Device that connects to a GoPro action camera for automated controls	5	End users connected to outdoor sports	Interviews and two surveys
Fashionder	Fashion app for smartphones that manages user's wardrobe	3	End user target group of young women	Interviews with potential users
Heartbeats	Wearable bracelets for communication by transmitting heartbeats	5	Jewelry purchasing end users	Interviews with jewelry shops and potential users
Drone In	Drones with projectors and social media for attracting young users	3	B2B service to event organizers	Conditional contracts from customers
Ham	Device for controlling and managing power usage of household appliances	3	B2B sales to SMEs	Interviewed German home appliances companies
HTH	Sensor based surgical implants that automatically warn users in case of failure	3	Selling through hospitals to customers	Contacted clinics and medical equipment manufacturers
iVend	Pluggable networked device to automatically manage and maintain vending machines	4	Current vending machine companies	Contacted vending machine companies and users
Columbus	Device to give tourists information on nearby monuments	5	Cities and tourism companies	Contacted city tourism offices
Jams	Modular wearable device that can adapt to user needs	5	Early tech adopting end user	Interviews with customers
Elevator 4.0	Pluggable networked device to manage and maintain elevators	4	Elevator maintainers Building owners	Interviews with elevator maintainers

4.3.2 Case Details for Sub-study 2

The second sub-study was a multiple case study with six cases on user innovations based on 3D printing found in online user communities. Open source communities in 3D design such as Thingiverse, have large collections of open source design files commonly stored in STL format. Each user design project or a "Thing" may consist of multiple designs that are viewable using a browser-based 3D viewer. Instructions, photos, and even videos of the final product often accompany them. A Thing may also contain non-3D printed components. These are often standard products and components available off the shelf and then used in the creation of the thing.

Users often used 3D printing in combination with open-source electronics hardware platforms to add utility to their innovations. The hardware consisted of a low-cost processor or micro-controller that users can easily program and with standard interfaces that connected to a large number of modular sensors and actuators. Users could combine these sensors and actuators with the processor to build innovative electronic prototypes such as home automation devices, simple robots, and even other 3D printers. The six cases are described in the following sections.

4.3.2.1 Case 1: Robohand Prosthetic Hand

Figure 7: Website screenshot of Robohand the 3D printed prosthetic hand

Robohand is a low-cost prosthetic hand developed by Richard, an artist, and woodworker from Johannesburg, South Africa with inputs from Ivan Owen, who often created theater props. There have been more than 200 hands developed and offered by him as a service as he moves on to design other innovations beneficial in his regions, such as solar-powered 3D printers, rugged battery backups, and even a Roboleg.

User Need: Richard lost fingers on his right hand in an accident and found out that commercial prosthetics were too expensive. He decided to design an alternative.

Design Process: Through constant pain that kept him up for days, he used his workshop and maker experience and constructed a prosthetic hand for himself. He soon collaborated with Ivan Owen who had worked on similar designs for building theater props. After a few trial and error cycles, and some exposure to 3D printing technologies, they developed an open source 3D design of Robohand. They first designed it in a workshop environment and then digitized it using general 3D design software and home printers. The first sign that they were reaching the end of their tunnel was when little Liam, a boy with a few missing fingers was fitted with a Robohand and he shouted out "It copies me!"

Innovative Product Created: Robohand has an open source design and consists of plastic 3D printed parts, medical Orthoplastic, and inexpensive materials that are available in a typical hardware store. It is a purely mechanical device without any electronics.

4.3.2.2 Case 2: Koruza Wireless Communication System

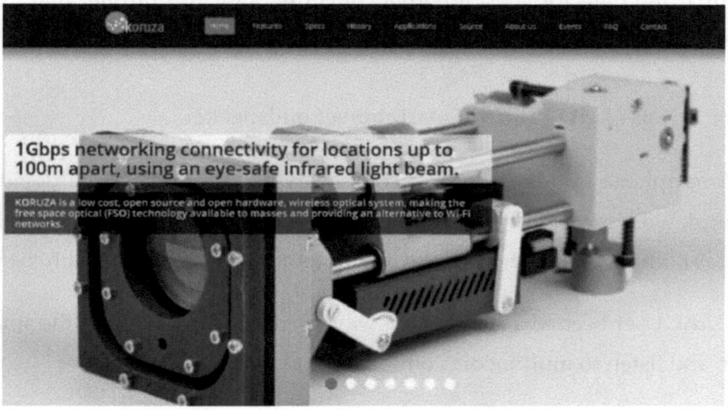

Figure 8: Website screenshot of Koruza wireless system

Koruza is an innovative open-source, open-hardware laser-based wireless communication system that can provide speeds of up to 1Gbps wirelessly, significantly faster than the current state of everyday fiber access networks. The capacity is sufficient to offer multi-user peer-to-peer daisy chain wireless connections and is ideal to provide last mile access as well internal area networks.

User Need: When Luka Mustafa or Musti for short, an enthusiast of decentralized ad-hoc networks was working on his student thesis, he stumbled upon an idea. He found that transmitting information over laser is significantly cheaper if the range is limited to a hundred meters. It gave him the idea of a point-to-point device that will promote a bottom-up organic network and be an alternative to traditional fiber and Wi-Fi networks.

Design Process: Musti used a 3D design tool with no specific solution space, but one that could give him the solution he wanted. The 3D printed parts, other components were refined through many iterations over the last year, and after four generations, it has transitioned from a large indoor system to a robust sleek outdoor system.

Innovative Product Created: It uses commoditized electronic components, such as a laser source and detector, lens, Ethernet converter, a microcontroller that formed the basic information interface along with 3D printed parts.

4.3.2.3 Case 3: 3D Printed Smartphone Loudspeaker

The Smartphone Loudspeaker is a completely 3D printed stylized device, purely mechanical, with no electronics. The device fits perfectly with a specified smartphone and acts as both as a smartphone stand as well as amplifying the smartphone speakers.

User Need: User needed a stand and a way to amplify the sound of the smartphone to watch and listen to multimedia comfortably.

Design Process: User is an experienced designer of CNC designs who migrated to designing for 3D printers. A MakerBot Replicator 2 printed out iterations of the design.

Figure 9: Screenshot of the 3D printed Smartphone Loudspeaker

Artifact Created: In this case, the product is an add-on by itself to the smartphone and hence has to have the necessary physical interface to integrate with the smartphone despite there being no interface from the smartphone side.

4.3.2.4 Case 4: Wii Wheel Gaming Add-on

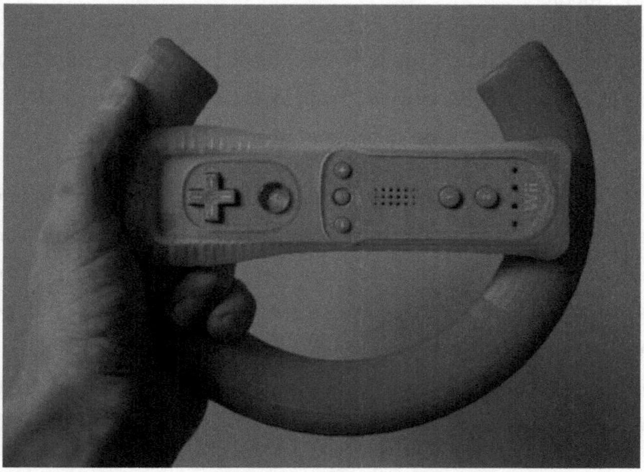

Figure 10: Screenshot of user published picture of the Wii Wheel

The Wii wheel is 3D printed with no electronics is also an add-on to the popular Wii motion-control gaming console from Nintendo for the special of playing racing video games.

User Need: User needed a racing wheel to play the game Mario Kart 8

Design Process: Simplify 3D made the design and a Felix 3.0 dual printer it out after a few iterations

Artifact Created: It looks and feels like a steering wheel but has a slot that exactly fits a Wii. Once again, the user innovator had to design a physical interface to this product so that it can add on to the Wii. The Wii, on the other hand, is quite sleek and does not have any physical features that promote extensions.

4.3.2.5 Case 5: Canedolly Time Lapse Camera Add-on

The Canedolly is an add-on to a digital camera; users can configure it to move the camera slowly along a guideway over a period so that it can record time-lapse videos.

User Need: for a specific user need of taking stylized time-lapse videos with smooth camera movements.

Design Process: An FDM printer built the plastic parts of the Canedolly. The metal rail was crafted using a metal saw and handiwork tools. Electronics were soldered in, and Arduino libraries were used to program the micro-controller.

Artifact Created: The Canedolly is a device that can be mounted on an uneven terrain and has a metal strip that acts as a track where the camera can be installed and an automated mechanism to guide the camera along the track over an extended period. It consists of standard parts from a hardware store such as screws, bolts, pulleys, belts tracks, and electronic hardware components such as motors, heat sinks, and Arduino microcontrollers. The Arduino and motor system are connected to the internal mechanisms of the camera to access its controls.

Figure 11: Screenshot of Canedolly for moving time-lapse pictures

4.3.2.6 Case 6: 4Track Robotic Vehicle

Thingiverse and Instructables have many user designs on remote controlled land and air based vehicles. The 4Track is one such user innovation that emphasizes having tracks and controllable claws.

User Need: To build low-cost robotics for hobby enthusiasts

Design Process: The user started out with making mechanical parts for a robot that moved with tracks. After five iterations and ten months of work, it resulted in an Arduino based robot with mechanical claws.

Artifact Created: Just like the exemplary Rover, in this case, the mechanical components are a combination of 3D printed parts such as the cylindrical wheels and the mechanical claw, along with standard screws and cables. The motors and sensors controlled by an Arduino microcontroller give it functionality. The Arduino platform and 3D design software were used to develop this product.

Figure 12: Screenshot of 4Track robot with claw

Having presented the case details for both studies, the next chapter presents the findings for the two sub-studies and findings from the cross-study analysis.

5 Findings

After conducting the two sub-studies that form this part, this chapter presents the major findings from the analyzed case data. The chapter consists of two sections. The first section presents the findings from the first sub-study, which is a single case study on a maker event themed around Internet of Things. This section focuses on collaboration activities observed during the event and design of their products. The second section presents findings from the second sub-study on multiple cases of user innovations in open source maker communities. The next chapter discusses these findings.

5.1 Findings from Sub-study 1

The first sub-study explored how users simplified their solution spaces when creating innovative solutions in the context of the early stages of building tangible products. It is a single case study on a two-week event to make innovative products using 3D printing and electronics. The goal of its participants was to collaboratively develop new ideas based on user needs, and develop them into functional prototypes while constantly evaluating prototype to meet user needs. As the period of the event was short but intensive, design processes that may have taken months occurred within the short time frame of the event.

The participants at first went through many ideation rounds and lightweight prototyping sessions to understand and to get familiar with the design thinking. They then identified user needs and further evaluated these needs by their interaction with potential users and industry experts. A participant summed up the experience as:

> *"I loved the design thinking talk as I found it detailed and really interesting, it gave me more to think about… I also really enjoyed the group task we did for building a quick prototype as it taught to think fast and try to be creative."* (EP1)

5.1.1 Modular Organization

The participants benefited from interacting in teams with mixed backgrounds that shared the large solution space available to them. They benefitted through guidance and resources they could find online as well as at the event. Talking to the mentors at the Academy and looking at their sample products helped the participants and gave the newcomers confidence and knowledge to use various tools and their solution spaces. One of the participants sums the feeling up with the following:

> *"When we started to prototype, we had big problems. However, with the help of my team, we got to a stage where together we are solving our problems and helping each other. We inspired each other to be better, to be motivated, and work effectively."* (EP2)

Working at the same location also allowed distribution of ideas and new solutions. The participants could regularly benchmark their teams against the other teams. It helped them gain solution information on intermediate designs as they heard each other pitch their ideas and demonstrated their prototypes every two or three days.

Working with technology that was open source was essential for the rapid prototyping and artifact development seen among the teams. It was quite evident that the ease of finding and reusing solutions in the form of learning resources and already developed software libraries online made development times very short. Initially, the participants chose a hardware toolkit whose solution space was familiar and an established online community supported:

> *"(...) my experience and technical skills, the teammates and of course forums and communities (...) Also, during my study I got a lot of information from googling and looking into forums ... for us they were flexible enough for (prototyping innovatively). The tools we had (sensors, interfaces, Arduinos) were easy and fast connectable and interfacable. Especially it is helpful that many libraries are downloadable for all the different sensors."* (EP3)

5.1.2 Modular Product Design

The products developed by the participants after the ideation phase were either working prototypes that showed technical capability or partially working replica devices that simulated the real product and demonstrated a new idea to get valuable user feedback. As the theme of the academy was IoT, the products contained electronic components. The participants built these products by combining different electronic sensors, actuators, and microcontrollers that could connect to the internet. The participants connected various modules of the platform as well other external products and the microcontroller acted as the informational interface between them. Using this modular electronics toolkit meant that design work was mostly substituting and augmenting modules in the system. Participants simplified their solution space by relying on existing hardware modules and creating new software programs and informational interfaces between them.

Modular toolkits with relatively smaller solution spaces like the Arduino platform were a popular choice as it was a modular toolkit for users. The participants could mix and match different modules and then quickly program the logic connecting them to get the necessary functionality. The reasoning behind their choice in the words of the participants is as follows:

"We had access to a wide range of tools made the prototyping easier and flexible" and *"the simplicity to use and configure the hardware device was also a parameter in order to take a decision on the choice of hardware."* (EP4)

The most basic Arduino board has an easily programmable microcontroller with input and output pins that easily connect to other electronic modules using wires and a breadboard. It was an ideal starting point for the development of many of the products. Once the electronics of the artifact were connected and functioning, the participants soldered them into place to make them more stable. The also assembled 3D printed or laser cut enclosures to house the electronics. After developing a first functioning prototype, teams either worked on optimizing the design by using smaller and more efficient and special purpose boards or added additional functionalities to make their prototype better suited for the market need. An overview of the ten teams and their products is in Table 7.

Table 7: Products, their design, and their components

Team Name	State of Product	Artifact Components	Tools Used
SensePro	Working Prototype with basic user evaluation	Interface to GoPro, gesture detection modules, Arduino, 3D printed box, custom software	Arduino based IDE, electronics, Tinkercad
Fashionder	Working Prototype with basic user evaluation	Smartphone with camera, barcode scanner module, mobile app	Barcode scanning libraries PHP
Heartbeats	Demonstration of Idea with functional components	Arduino mini, vibrator module, heart rate sensor, Bluetooth modules, 3D printed bracelets	Tinkercad Arduino modules
Drone In	Demonstration of Idea without functional components	Drone, projector	Drone assembler kit
Ham	Working Prototype with basic user evaluation	PCB with microcontroller, Wi-Fi, power electronics, cloud-based app for smartphones	Advanced electronics PCB modeling software
HTH	Demonstration of Idea without functional components	3D printed bone (to demonstrate implant's location), Ultrasonic sensors (to demonstrate principle)	3D design downloaded Arduino modules Ultrasonic Sensor
iVend	Demonstration of Idea with functional components	3D printed case, breadboard, and Arduino, infra-red sensor, display	Tinkercad Arduino modules
Columbus	Demonstration of Idea with functional components	Mobile App, Bluetooth low energy beacons, Arduino	Arduino IDE
Jams	Working Prototype with basic user evaluation	3D printed clip-on cases, Arduino mini based modules for each Jam, innovative bus system for connecting modules	Arduino, soldering tools, electronics, Tinkercad
Elevator 4.0	Working Prototype with basic user evaluation	Arduino, Distance sensors, laser cut box for casing, display, Wi-Fi	Arduino IDE adobe Photoshop, laser cutter

5.2 Findings from Sub-study 2

The findings of the second sub-study on user innovations based on 3D printing found in online user communities are presented here. In these cases of user innovations in open source communities, users had gained knowledge through either formal studies or their hobbies and work experiences, but they were not particularly trained in this area. Although the products they developed may have been commercially available, they often were too expensive or constraining. As one of the interviewees expressed:

"I designed them a few years ago when I was in university (studying electronics and robotics). I wanted to program robots and develop path-planning algorithms, but commercial, educational robots for universities are extremely expensive and hard to come by. Designing my own printable robots allowed me to make custom parts and reduce the cost!" (UI1)

The users also had very specific needs that existing products did not satisfactorily meet. They were unsatisfied with the existing products in the market and sought to create their own. As a user innovator mentions:

"And I started investigating things online, and all the different prosthetics that are available, and none of them are trade friendly, and none of them are functional as in returning functionality to your hand as a tradesman." (UI3)

5.2.1 Modular Organization

The user innovators from the hardware open source communities studied began by working on their innovative ideas independently and shared their designs in online platforms like Thingiverse and Instructables. The user innovation cases sampled in the study are of designs that went farthest and emerged as dominant designs. However, users also received some assistance in this process. Other users contributed, by sharing the design process and hence simplifying solution space by commenting on each other's projects and suggesting ideas. On a much smaller scale, they made derivatives of the designs by forking out published designs and made their own versions of them or specialized on different parts.

Collaboration to simplify solution space was, however, not restricted to the user community platforms as in the case of Robohand. After Richard the founder had first built a few prototypes at his workshop, he then contacted Ivan over email after watching a video of him on the social media site YouTube, showing a large mechanical hand that he used as a movie prop. Ivan, in turn, got the idea of using a consumer 3D printer to lower the cost of designing the components from a colleague.

As others began to perceive that the user innovations captured needs of society, the innovations caught their interest and they slowly became part of the community and contributed by communicating to the user in discussions. Discussions were in the form of comments on the platforms as well as websites and blogs of the user innovators. For example, Ivan Oven who built mechanical hands as theater and cinema props also contributed to Robohand. Users credited the open source development approach to the success of some of their projects. Ivan says that it enabled collaboration between a diverse set of individuals:

"As a tool for open source development; this makes it possible for people from a wide range of experiences and backgrounds to collaborate with one another. You can have everyone in the mix from people who have their PhDs in material science to people who are tinkering in the garage." (UI3)

5.2.1.1 Community Funding

An interesting finding that emerged was that crowdfunding played a major part in the case of Koruza and Robohand. Luka Mustafa from Koruza used a successful crowd funding campaign to present his design at the American Conference on Information Systems (AMCIS) where he received valuable feedback for his design and attracted potential collaborators. He later won a fellowship that allowed active development with a dedicated team. Robohand also started a crowdfunding campaign to purchase some basic tools that helped them get started. They also received further aid from the 3D printing firm Makerbot:

"I decided to give it a try and send Makerbot an email. I let them know what we were up to and asked them if they were able to help in any way or even provide us with a machine or two to use. I saw this as a long shot. We have no background in this field, we have no

credentials, and will you please send us two of your very high tech machines for free. Much to our surprise and delight, they responded extremely positively. They were supportive and encouraging of what we were trying to accomplish and even provided us with two of their printers to attempt to develop the design." (UI3)

5.2.1.2 Sharing user innovations

The user innovators publish their innovations in these platforms after they have developed working prototypes rather than share work in progress designs. Publishing the designs on the online platforms often happened at a much later stage when there was a working prototype ready. Users publish their user innovations in the form of editable 3D design files, in an open format such as STL, a list of standard hardware and electronic parts, downloadable software and a manual consisting of steps needed to reproduce the innovation.

5.2.1.3 Modularity-in-production with 3D Printing

Using 3D printing technologies to cut costs in designing custom components was the initial motivation of the users. However, as they started using this technology, additional benefits became clear. Users could print out multiple copies that were exact physical representations of a 3D design. It encouraged users to collaborate when jointly working on a product. Ivan aptly put across this point in the case of Robohand:

"We were able to print out the same component, get on video chat and when holding the same object, even though we were so far apart, look at it, explore, brainstorm and make those changes, email each other the files, and then reprint and start the process over again." (UI3)

"It was an incredible boost to the speed of the design process, much along the lines of stepping out of a horse drawn carriage and immediately hopping into a formula one racer." (UI3)

The technology reduced time for trial and error cycles of visualizing a new design and printing it. The reduced trial and error cycles enabled users to make many iterations in design, in some cases vastly go further than the initial plan of the design, and achieve much more. A large number of design versions and variations and the following statement from Jon of 4Track emphasize this point:

> *"I started out by making a very simple tracked robot (Caterpillar) and later combined four of these to make a much larger and complex robot (4Track). The whole process took several months (10 months) and many changes, so the end result was very different to what I had imagined in the beginning."* (UI4)

The users worked on commercial 3D printers for home use such as the printers from Makerbot that were relatively inexpensive when compared to professional 3D printers and printed in different types of plastic. OpenSCAD was a favorite design tool as it was easy to build 3D designs based on geometrical shapes for functional purposes. Therefore, users chose toolkits with a sufficiently broad solution space to design functional shapes. There was an emphasis on a 3D printer that had excellent print quality, high reliability and safety, which was plug & play and easy to use. In the case of Koruza and Robohand when the commercial printer needed further feature improvements, they either modified the printer or made printers themselves. Richard, for example, has also developed a 3D printer called Robobeast. It has a design optimized for rugged conditions with features like a backup battery and solar panels that are suitable for outdoor printing.

5.2.2 Modular Product Design

The innovative products consisted of 3D printed parts, off-the-shelf products that users can purchase in a hardware store, and as in the case of electronic products, low-cost electronic components such as sensors, actuators, and microcontrollers. They used standard hardware components whenever 3D printed parts did not meet physical and functional requirements of the artifact. They used the solution space of 3D printing to create 3D printed parts that physically connected other parts for e.g. casing for electronics. The solution space of low-cost microcontrollers like Arduino enabled processing of information and interfacing between other electronic components. Table 8 presents the components used in all the six products. The words of one of the interviewees summarized the use of solution space by users very well:

"The 3D printed parts are often designed around the standard parts, and the low-cost modular electronics platforms such as Arduino were like the ***glue*** *that connected the other parts".* (UI2)

Table 8: Products designed and their components

Case	3D printed Parts	Standard Parts	Electronics
Robohand	Finger and palm area of prosthetic hand with screw holes	Screws, Orthoplastic material in contact with skin, nylon cables	-None-
Koruza	Frames, stands, casings	Screws, waterproof casings	Micro-controller, laser transmitter, and receiver, Ethernet card
Smart Phone Speaker	3D printed speaker with socket	-None-	-None-
Wii wheel	3D printed wheel with socket	-None-	-None-
4Track	Wheels, body, casings, mechanical arm	Screws, rubber bands	Micro-controller, sensors, and motors
Cane Dolly	Adjustable legs, casing, stand for camera	Screws, metal rail	Micro-controller, motor, and wiring

5.3 Cross Findings from Sub-studies

5.3.1 Stages of User Innovation

The two sub-studies provide valuable insights on the process followed by user innovators making innovative products. The users in the first sub-study on the maker event followed the early stages of this process and outlined a plan for the future. The users in the second sub-study developed their products over a period of 6-12 months. The stages identified in both the sub-studies were consolidated and modeled into a 4-step process that users followed. Figure 13 presents the process model.

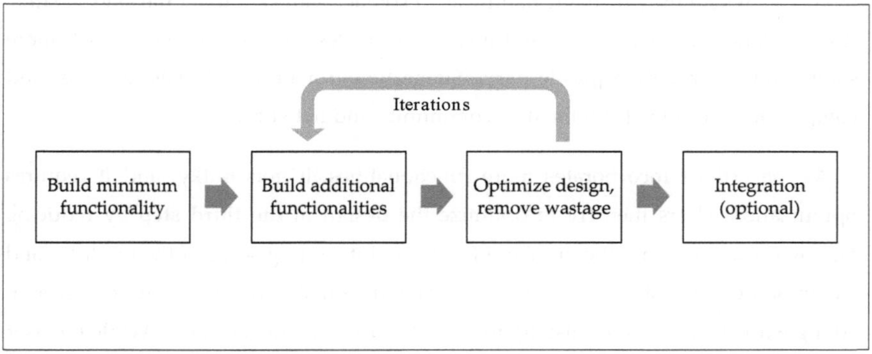

Figure 13: Stages of the user innovation process for tangible products

The first step was to build an artifact that implemented the core functionality they had identified, which could act as a solution to the needs identified. Their solution information was initially restricted to their educational or professional backgrounds that were often specialized to one discipline and some basic design experiences. Because of this restriction, users often started designing with toolkits that had enough solution space to implement a first working prototype. For mechanical parts, this could be in the form of crude 3D prints or parts that were fashioned in a workshop. These parts needed to have the necessary shape to make the first prototype work. Electronic parts often were prototyping electronics like Arduino modules, plugged to breadboards and connected to each other with jumper wires. This limitation was also in software, with just the basic implementation of necessary functions. When the available solution space was not enough, users reduced their scope of their needs or simply altered them to match what they could design.

Once they created the first working prototype, **the second step** was to include other functionalities into the artifact they needed before the artifact could be operational in a real or simulated environment. Such functionalities may include: the stable connection between various components, casings for electronics, using materials the right strength, etc. Parts from hardware stores may have superior physical properties (strength, weight, shape, etc.) to 3D printed plastic parts, which make them necessary to operationalize the prototype. Robohand, for example, used Orthoplastic material at the points where the prosthetic hand was in contact with skin to let the skin breathe. It used standard metal screws and bolts in these designs, as they were much more stable and reliable than plastic parts. Suggestions for new materials, designs, and components can come from the user community and network.

As the artifact incorporates more functionalities, it gets bulky, and it requires optimization. Users then try to optimize the design in **the third step** by reducing wastage. They decrease the number of parts by integrating some of the modules and streamlining 3D designs with reduced material to make the artifact more efficient. Along with efficiency, they also try to make the artifact more aesthetic. While the user innovators may not always be directly designing to appeal to others, they have a strong sense of how their designs should appear and appreciate positive feedback from others. Over time as the user innovator increases solution information, starts using more advanced toolkits and may reduce reliance on standard parts.

Most of the cases of user innovators iterate between steps two and three as they keep improving their products by either adding newer functionalities or optimizing their design. In the case of Koruza, after three years of developing the artifact, it was preparing to go into production as **the fourth step**. It marked a departure from the earlier design approach where the artifact consisted of modular parts that users could easily purchase or 3D print. Koruza plans to branch their design to have two parallel design versions. One design is for production, and the other will continue as a modular design for makers to develop further. The production version will further integrate the design to lower costs and make it available in the market.

5.3.2 Dynamic Interfaces to Simplify Solution Space

As mentioned earlier, many user innovations did not restrict themselves to one solution space for their creations but rather often used multiple solution spaces that best fit their needs. Users used multiple toolkits from different fields that included machining tools, 3D printing tools, as well as modular electronic systems.

User innovated products ranged from modifications to new products built out of existing off-the-shelf items. Some of these were components, while others were standalone products, not designed to be connected to other products. In these cases, the products did not have necessary interfaces to treat them as components and connect them to other products. User innovators instead built their *dynamic interfaces* to connect these products. In some cases, user innovators insisted on developing everything from scratch. However, as the products grew more complex, they were often designed as add-ons to existing products than new products from scratch.

They used toolkits that gave them sufficiently large solution space to create interfaces dynamically. These dynamic interfaces could either be hard interfaces, mechanical in nature or soft interfaces that were informational in nature. 3D printing toolkits allowed users to build hard interfaces between products, such as slots, gears, clips, tracks, etc. Low-cost computing in the form of microcontrollers created programmable soft interfaces for information transfer different electronic components. Thus, these dynamic interfaces may be electronic in nature by connecting different input-output pins, transferring and translating information, or mechanical in nature by having matching right shapes and connections that users could dynamically design using additive manufacturing or 3D printing technology.

Both these types of dynamic interfaces reflect the digitization of hardware, where mechanical components are software design files and software applications in an embedded system. While these methods would traditionally be expensive or inaccessible, the reducing cost of both 3D printing and computing allows user innovators to use a computer or a 3D printed part as links between systems rather than the central system itself.

6 Discussion

This chapter discusses the findings from both the sub-studies and the cross-study analysis in the previous chapter. The first sub-study is a single case study on a maker event on Internet of Things, where participants with multiple toolkits and associated solution spaces designed innovative solutions based on their estimated needs over a period of around two weeks. The second sub-study consisted of multiple cases on user innovations in open source maker communities and described how users developed their innovative solutions from the various solution spaces to design they have access to, in the form of open hardware electronics, 3D printing, etc. The second sub-study complemented the findings of the first. Together, they provided the advantage of observing the development process up close and identifying mechanisms for simplifying solution space in both nascent as well as established user innovations. The section below discusses the overall findings from both the sub-studies.

6.1 Solution Space for User Innovation

The empirical context of the two sub-studies on user innovators involved in 'making' differs from previous work on user innovators organized in communities. User innovation communities have been discussed around large open source projects such as in Linux operating system or Apache software (Harhoff et al., 2003; Lakhani & Von Hippel, 2003) or in open hardware (Balka et al., 2009; Raasch et al., 2009) mentioned in Chapter 2. Instead, the users in these two sub-studies were part of smaller projects (one to five members), some of which attracted external contributions only after a duration of around six months. These users can be considered lead users who went beyond describing problems, stating needs or even suggesting solutions to organizing among each other and developing the solutions (Mahr & Lievens, 2012).

The two sub-studies applied theory on modular organizations to the separation of design process between firms and users and between users' themselves (Schilling, 2000). Modularity in product design was a core component in the user innovations, and it allowed decentralization of the design process and its management (Sanchez & Mahoney, 1996).

In the studied cases, users shared the design workload through various forms of modularity-in-design, by working with other users or reusing existing products with embedded design. Existing products with embedded design are dynamically integrated with each other by a combination of splitting, augmentation and linking operators (Baldwin & Clark, 2001). Dynamic interfaces in this study are developed in the decentralized and ad-hoc approach which make them different from the concept of 'systems integrators' (Brusoni & Prencipe, 2001). The creation of interfaces "on-demand" to integrate different modular system hence is a new outcome of these technologies.

6.2 Conclusion

Part II of the thesis has studied user-innovators in online maker communities and in an offline maker event to understand how users simplify solution space when creating innovative products. It describes two sub-studies and presents their findings. The findings show that user innovators varied in their approaches to developing solution information based on their knowledge and availability of tools and technologies. However, these approaches changed with time as they developed their expertise and further clarified their need information. Non-expert users can learn from this behavior and start with toolkits that offer the minimum necessary solution space to build their first prototypes, while gradually expanding to more advanced toolkits. The advanced toolkits give them the solution space needed to develop specific solutions for their specific needs.

The user innovations in the two sub-studies were often add-ons to larger products or novel combinations of existing products. It was another approach of using embedded design knowledge to simplify users' solution space to design. It was possible by building their dynamic interfaces that adapted to existing products, which were either, or both: 3D printed hard interfaces or soft interfaces programmed on embedded systems.

Part III

Structuring Solution Space:

Exploring Toolkits Simplifying Solution Space

1 Needs and Objectives

The previous Part of the dissertation explored how user innovators simplified their solution space for creating innovative solutions. It looked at solution space of the user, where the user may use multiple toolkits and work with various solution spaces. This study contributes to the overall research question of the dissertation by exploring the *inner structure* of toolkit solution space (Simon, 1969). The inner structure consists of the architecture and composition of the toolkit and can be analyzed by studying *the artifacts* themselves (Chatterjee, 2015), i.e., by studying toolkits and their solution spaces. *Part III*[17] explores how toolkits simplify solution space for non-expert users. As it narrows the focus down, from the user's solution space with multiple toolkits to a single toolkit's solution space, it is a natural progression from *Part II* and is complementary to it.

As was mentioned earlier, 3D printing and other digital fabrication technologies have brought considerable production flexibility into the hands of users. Through these technologies, users can physically produce items in any 3D shape imaginable. Low-end consumer 3D printers are limited in the quality of products and the scope of materials they can print with. Firms who offer digital fabrication services (Bull & Groves, 2009) on the other hand, allow users to produce items in a variety of materials such as various plastics, glass, ceramic, metal, etc. (Dimitrov et al., 2006)

Users can utilize this significant design freedom or solution space to innovate and design, through advanced computer-aided design (CAD) software. However, CAD software can be considered as advanced toolkits for user innovation and design (von Hippel & Katz, 2002) that require a lot of user involvement, thus restricting them to expert users. The average user who cannot put in as much time and effort to get involved with learning-by-doing needs "basic toolkits" with smaller solution spaces (Prügl & Schreier, 2006). A basic toolkit is used for product customization and

---

[17] Earlier versions of this research have been presented at the Open and User Innovation Conference (OUI) 2013 as (Naik & Möslein, 2013) and European Conference on Information Systems (ECIS) 2016 as (Naik, Velamuri, & Möslein, 2016)

individualization (Franke & Schreier, 2002). The small solution space, allows limited elicitation of only relevant user preferences, thus striking the right balance between flexibility and ease of use (Franke & Schreier, 2002; Zipkin, 1997). Basic toolkits in the context of 3D printing are often easy to use web applications that allow users to customize existing products by changing a few parameters (e.g., a customizable finger ring with different sizes and patterns as is shown in Figure 14). Such toolkits require lesser user involvement than CAD software but are heavily restricted in the products they can create.

Defining the solution space of a toolkit for non-expert users is not straightforward when users' needs are too heterogeneous. For example, the 'Sake Set Creator' app in Figure 1 can be used to design and manufacture customized Sake themed crockery using 3D printing. This toolkit allows users to visualize the product in three dimensions, and the solution space is restricted to creating cylindrically symmetrical shapes. However, users who need to create something other than a Sake Set will not have their needs met. These needs are outside the solution space of the toolkit even when they are well within the production capabilities of the firm. Thus, the basic toolkit aimed at non-expert users is not sufficient for heterogeneous user demand, and it offers only a part of the capabilities of a 3D printer to its users.

Research in other contexts of toolkits for user innovation and design also identified this problem. In a study that developed toolkits for innovation in the context of shopping centers, it was found that development of solution space and module libraries needed to be open to users (Helminen et al., 2015). Research calls for the further democratization of innovation, as most studies on user innovation toolkits address expert users, while toolkits for non-expert users have been limited to customization rather than for innovation (Goduscheit & Jørgensen, 2013). Hence, this study explores empirical cases of toolkits in the context of 3D Printing, where there is a large potential solution space that toolkits can simplify to enable non-expert users to innovate and design.

RQ2: How do toolkits for user innovation and design simplify solution space for non-expert users?

The study follows a multiple case study approach to systematically explore and analyze a sample of contemporary 3D printing toolkits and identify mechanisms in these toolkits to simplify solution space. After systematically searching through publicly available 3D design software, a sample of 68 3D printing toolkits eligible for the study was selected. These 68 3D printing toolkits and related data were used to construct a database of 68 cases of toolkits in 3D printing. The cases were built using theory on modular systems for analyzing toolkit solution space (Baldwin & Clark, 2004). The solution spaces of toolkits were categorized in terms of the design questions that users have to answer when designing with the toolkit and their respective design options. The cases were analyzed using this categorization and modularity-in-design to identify different mechanisms found in toolkits to simplify solution space for non-expert users.

The study found four mechanisms that simplify solution space for non-expert users. These mechanisms are the following: Firstly, offering known design questions with known design options that iteratively create complex designs. Secondly, by using generative algorithms which generate complex designs with minimal input. Thirdly, by enabling users to reuse existing designs from other users or services. Fourthly, offering 'meta-toolkits' for users to create their own toolkits so that users can share the design complexity among themselves. The opening of toolkit creation to users is highlighted, as this extends the idea of openness (Chesbrough, 2003) of toolkits by bringing ideas to design solution spaces from outside the firm.

The rest of Part III has the following structure: It begins by setting the appropriate context with background literature on toolkits for user innovation and design. An explanation of the theoretical framework used for the study. The next chapter is the detailed research design and methodology used for the multiple case study. The categorization of toolkit solution space and the identified mechanisms for simplifying solution space for non-expert users constitute the findings of the study. It ends with a chapter discussing the findings and their implications.

Nervous System Cell Cycle: Nervous System is a firm that aims to work at the intersection of science, art, and technology. They generate designs from computer simulations that draw inspiration from phenomena found in nature and use digital fabrication to realize products out of these designs. They also offer web-based toolkits to customers who can create their own, unique and affordable art, jewelry, and housewares and release their source code under a creative commons license to encourage others to extend their work[18]. *Cell Cycle* shown with a screenshot below is an example of one of these toolkits, which can design rings, bangles, cuffs, or sculptures using generated designs that are inspired by cellular structures. Users can customize the design by changing its dimensions and aesthetically tweaking parameters that feed into the cellular structure generation.

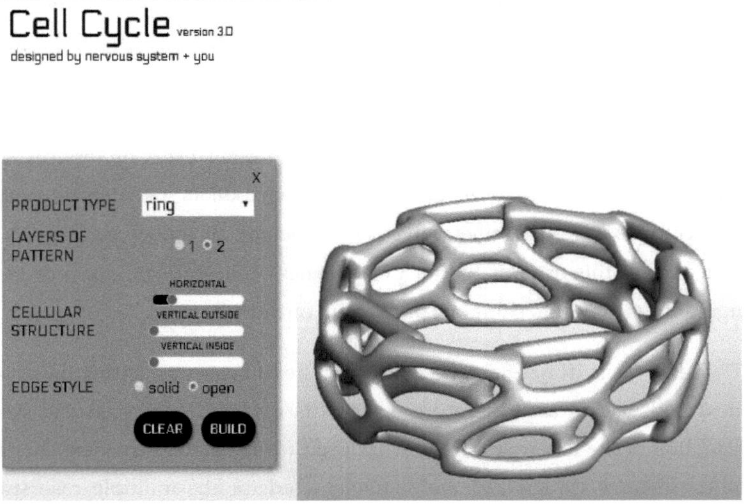

Figure 14: Screenshots of Cell Cycle, toolkit for customizable 3D printed rings

[18] Nervous System has other design toolkits and a large collection of generated designs (http://n-e-r-v-o-u-s.com accessed on 2015-09-12).

2 Understanding the Context

Integrating user innovation and design ideas requires a bridge between the problem information found among users and the solution information, which a firm can provide. Use of information systems can minimize the interaction and information cost arising in this process. These systems are toolkits for user innovation and design, coordinated sets of design tools that enable users to develop new product innovations and designs themselves (Franke & Schreier, 2002; von Hippel & Katz, 2002). As the study focusses on solution space, it uses the Franke and Schreier classification (Franke & Schreier, 2002) of toolkits into expert toolkits and basic toolkits based on the degree of innovation freedom offered to users and omit toolkits for idea competitions (Piller & Walcher, 2006) from this study. The following sections describe expert and basic toolkits.

2.1 Expert toolkits

Expert toolkits or high-end toolkits are a source of radical innovations as they offer virtually all the solution space within the manufacturer's production capabilities to users. Thus they tend to be more challenging to use and demand greater user skill (Prügl & Schreier, 2006). Lead users apply expert toolkits to significantly alter a product or even develop a new product to meet needs that existing products do not meet.

Firms have used expert toolkits to 'plant' and 'grow' innovators among their user base. Expert users using the toolkit have developed modules, which firms later incorporated into the standard versions of the products after the firms found these modules to be popular and error free. Examples include the case of the statistical analysis software firm 'Stata,' the case of toolkits for the game 'The Sims' and toolkits of the virtual world 'Second Life' (Franke & Schreier, 2002; Kohler, Matzler, & Füller, 2009; Prügl & Schreier, 2006). The study on toolkits used in 'The Sims' provides an instance where expert users are not content with the official toolkits provided by the manufacturer, and often create and use their own toolkits to further push the design possibilities. Furthermore, the use of these toolkits is not restricted to their creators but also have a high demand among other users as well.

Expert toolkits have also equipped other users to contribute in product design without having all the necessary skills to design a product from scratch. Toolkits that provide libraries (of options or modules) let users convert their innovative ideas into products by combining different modules. Furthermore, expert toolkits also benefit lead users by reducing person-hours required for creating new product designs. Modularity makes it easier for lead users to focus and develop product functions without having to redesign the whole product. Thus, individual users can also develop complex products, traditionally designed by large teams, by using modular designed toolkits (Baldwin & Clark, 2004).

2.2 Basic toolkits

While large solution spaces give users the capability to innovate, small solution spaces are typically sufficient for customization. Basic toolkits (Prügl & Schreier, 2006) are toolkits with small solution spaces used to elicit customer preferences and include them into the product design. These systems have been called configurators, choice boards, design systems, or co-design platforms (Franke & Piller, 2003; Piller, 2005). Toolkits cater to highly heterogeneous demand where users have considerable diversity in their preferences. These users are willing to pay a premium for both customized and innovative products, as can be seen in Apache's security software, mass customized watches, personalized apparel, etc. (Franke & Piller, 2003, 2004; Franke & Schreier, 2010; Franke & von Hippel, 2003; Piller, 2005).

Even before 3D printing and other digital fabrication technologies, improved production processes, and manufacturing systems have enabled firms to produce individualized goods at near mass-product efficiency (Dimitrov et al., 2006; Tseng & Jiao, 1996). However, they often offer a small solution space because of constraints in the production process. The solution space is also restricted in other cases to find the right balance between flexibility and ease of use. Therefore, such toolkits tend to be very user-friendly and demand less effort from users to operate (Prügl & Schreier, 2006).

Basic toolkits are designed to be very easy to use to reduce the interaction costs in designing the products as average users are willing to only invest in design if the benefits of an individualized product exceed the costs associated with creating it (Franke & von Hippel, 2003; von Hippel, 1994). User friendliness is maintained with an emphasis on low perceived complexity, which is often achieved by restricting the solution space of the toolkit (Dellaert & Stremersch, 2005; Salvador et al., 2009). Such toolkits are usually configurators, where users configure their products across a limited number of dimensions.

Table 9: Toolkits for user innovation and design in literature

	Toolkit Objectives	**Empirical Field**
Expert Toolkits	Motivate and capture innovations from external consumer community (L. B. Jeppesen & Molin, 2003)	Computer Games
	Facilitate problem-solving and aid diffusion of toolkit related information with community (L. B. Jeppesen, 2005)	Computer Games
	Training inexperienced non-expert users to leading innovative users (Prügl & Schreier, 2006)	Computer Games
	Convert user community to a firm asset (L. B. Jeppesen & Frederiksen, 2006)	Music Instruments
	Co-creation experience around the toolkit (Kohler, Fueller, Stieger, & Matzler, 2011; Kohler et al., 2009; Thomas Kohler, Johann Fueller, Kurt Matzler, & Daniel Stieger, 2011)	Virtual Worlds
	Identifying innovative users and innovation communication (Hung, Chou, & Dong, 2011)	Social networking
	Develop new services (Kankanhalli et al., 2015)	Mobile Apps
Basic Toolkits	User satisfaction through customization (Franke & von Hippel, 2003)	Server Software
	Higher willingness to pay (WTP) for self-designed products (Franke & Piller, 2004)	Watches
	Peer assistance in mass customization toolkits improved problem-solving behavior (Franke, Keinz, & Schreier, 2008)	Carving Skis
	Customers have higher WTP when they know what they want (Franke, Keinz, & Steger, 2009)	Newspapers, fountain pens, kitchens, skis, and breakfast cereals
	"I designed it myself" effect creates economic value (Franke, Schreier, & Kaiser, 2010)	Scarves, T-shirts, cell phone covers, skis, and watches

2.3 Solution Space Development

Toolkit solution space was in the past restricted by limits of flexibility in the production process, but these limits have broadened as new production processes, and manufacturing systems have enabled firms to produce individualized goods at near mass-product efficiency (Dimitrov et al., 2006; Tseng & Jiao, 1996). Some of the first methods for developing solution space include (a) analyzing existing consumer products and determining the dimensions required to design them, (b) making existing in-house design tools if any user-friendly or (c) using feedback from lead users. The solution space could then be fine-tuned by recording and observing usage patterns in the toolkits (von Hippel & Katz, 2002).

Solution space in basic toolkits is often restricted, to keep a balance between design flexibility and perceived ease-of-use for the user (Dellaert & Stremersch, 2005; Salvador et al., 2009). There is a trade-off between the design effort required to use the toolkit (Zipkin, 1997) and retrieving specific customer preferences, while keeping the toolkit user-friendly (Prügl & Schreier, 2006; Randall et al., 2005). At the same time, solution space with a minimal design effort gives users the "I designed it myself" feeling while designing their products (Franke et al., 2010).

In basic toolkits that work as configurators, solution space is in the form of configurable options in the toolkit. There can be a discrete number of options from which the user selects an option, or a potentially infinite range where users can enter their exact preference (e.g., a text field or a picture upload option) (Huffman & Kahn, 1998; von Hippel & Katz, 2002). Randall et al. (2007) emphasize on offering a design parameter toolkit with exact product parameters to expert users while providing a need-based toolkit (based on user needs) to non-expert users. In the case of a need-based toolkit, providing a high 'preference fit' of users to their needs is preferred (Huffman & Kahn, 1998). These user needs or preferences are characterized along three dimensions: fit, functionality and aesthetic design (Piller, 2005).

Hermans has proposed a model for evaluating solution space of basic toolkits based on an experiential creation by Dahl & Moreau. The model interprets customization as a creative task and has two dimensions: Firstly, the level at which the solution space dictates the target outcome. It can be regarding the type of customizable product attributes, mechanisms for customization and amount of choice. Secondly, the amount of guidance provided to the user in creating an outcome. It is in the form of different starting points in the customization process, guiding method, instructions to the user and feedback on the process (Hermans, 2012, 2014).

As can be seen above, literature has researched solution space of basic toolkits (customization). However, in the context of 3D printing, solution space is large and has a wide range, from customizing products to designing innovative products. Simplifying solution space has to be researched as a whole in this context. Simplifying the solution space offered by 3D printing is significant in this regard and presents a challenge for both expert toolkits (innovation) and basic toolkits (customization). For an expert toolkit, solution space has to be broken down into appropriate, simplified design decisions that encourage non-expert users as well. For basic toolkits, solution space needs to cater to heterogeneous demand from users that may otherwise fall out of their scope.

3 Theoretical Underpinning

This chapter describes the theoretical underpinning of the study. The study uses modularity theory that *Part I* and *Part II* introduced earlier, with a focus on modularity to study solution spaces of toolkits and their simplification. As toolkits by definition consist of modular libraries, theory on modular systems is an appropriate perspective to study toolkit solution space. Furthermore, modularization manages complexity (Baldwin & Clark, 2001, 2004) making it suitable for the research problem on how toolkit solution space is simplified. Two principles of modularity are relevant for this study. The first is modularity-in-use as users mix and match elements at each level of the solution space to build their final product that suits their tastes and needs. The second is modularity-in-design as the process of design is split up by the toolkit into separate modules that are operated by separate entities (users, manufacturers, etc.), which are coordinated by design rules. The rest of this chapter discusses both these types of modularity further in the context of toolkit solution space.

3.1 Modularity-in-use

When users design, they make design decisions where they select an option for each design question. Users make these design decisions when they use a functionality of the toolkit. It can be in the form of selecting from a drop down list, a checkbox or entering into a text field. It is akin to mixing and matching elements, where each option was chosen an element selected for that level of the solution space. As users mix and match elements at different levels of the toolkit solution space to build their products, they are following the principle of modularity-in-use. They design products by 'using' different design options for each level of design questions offered by the toolkit.

To more formally understand design decisions of modularity-in-use, the terminology of 'Questions' and 'Options' is adopted from design space analysis (MacLean, Young, Bellotti, & Moran, 1991). Design space analysis provides the rationale behind the design of an artifact, explaining not only the design of the artifact but also the reasons behind why it was designed exactly in that manner. As toolkits design artifacts, their solution space can be modeled using elements of design space analysis.

Design space analysis uses a simple notation called QOC that represents the basic concepts of decision space analysis. These are 1) Questions, which are the key design issues for the product; 2) Options, which are the possible answers to each design question; and 3) Criteria, which are the basis for evaluating and choosing among the options. Using this notation, the product design is a series of 'QOC steps.' These steps may also be included along with the product itself as a 'co-product of design.' Table 10 explains the QOC notation using an example of a simple 3D printed cufflinks that has been developed using the "Round Cufflinks" customizer from Mixeelabs.

Table 10: QOC model for designing with the "Round Cufflinks" toolkit

Design Questions	*Design Options*	*Design Criteria*
What are the different elements of the cufflinks customized?	**What options does each design question have?**	**What are the criteria for selecting an option?**
What material do the cufflinks have?	Steel, Silver, SLS Nylon Plastic	Has to be inexpensive
What is the color/finishing?	Steel, Gold Plated, Bronze Plated	Needs to fit formal occasions
What is etched?	Text or graphic	Personalized with users name
What text is added?	Any text can be entered	Personalized with users name
How is the text positioned?	Along the surface of the cufflinks	Aesthetically placed
What size is the text?	XS, S, M, L, XL	The final design should be aesthetic

Each design function or parameterized attribute in the toolkit is a design question. The user effectively 'selects' an option by choosing an attribute or applying the design function in a specific manner. The design questions and design options are limited by taking into account constraints of production and required user involvement. The criteria of users may also be influenced by highlighting certain options over others to make it easier for non-expert users (Randall et al., 2005). For each design question, the design options can be further analyzed by looking at whether they are addressing maximizing or satisficing behaviors in users (Simon, 1956). Toolkits with not too many design questions and the standard list of design options may be directed to satisficing users. They offer users a lower aspirational level and a higher cost of designing their products, thus making them easier to satisfy by toolkits with limited design questions and options (i.e. satisficing behavior). Toolkits with design questions that allow users to set the exact option they need are aimed towards maximizing users.

3.2 Modularity-in-design

As the user designs a product with a toolkit, the process of design has contributions from both the user as well as the toolkit maker. Hence, toolkits split the process of design and distribute it across separate modules, leading to the principle of modularity-in-design. Furthermore, these 'modules' of contribution are coordinated by design rules enforced by the toolkit rather than by direct coordination between users and manufacturers (Baldwin & Clark, 2004). Toolkit makers contribute to their module of product design and set the design rules for coordinating with users' modules of product design. These design rules are often enforced by limiting toolkit solution space to the allowed design rules of the toolkit maker (von Hippel & Katz, 2002). The study can explore where from and how design contributions come from when using each toolkit by applying this perspective. It also leads to the theory of modular organizations (Schilling, 2000; Schilling & Steensma, 2001) which emerge in the highly networked additive manufacturing industry.

Table 11: Modularity-in-use and Modularity-in-design for toolkit solution space

Modularity-in-use	**Modularity-in-design**
• Users mix and match elements to design their products • Involves choosing a design option for each design question • Design questions and options are imbibed in toolkit solution space	• Final product design shared across different entities • Design modules connected by design rules • Design rules can be in the form of toolkit design questions and options

Hence, these principles of modularity and related theory on design spaces serve as a theory to analyze toolkit solution spaces empirically. The study used this theory to analyze cases on toolkit solution space, with the aim of exploring and identifying mechanisms found in toolkits that simplify solution space for the non-expert user. The next chapter presents the research method used in this study with a detailed research design and the data for the cases.

4 Method and Data

This chapter presents the method and data used in the study to explore and identify how toolkits simplify solution space for non-expert users. The chapter consists of three sections. The first section places the research approach followed in *Part III* in the overall research approach of the thesis. The second section describes the research design by explaining in detail the method used, empirical data, data collection processes, and data analysis. The third section describes the data sample, which consists of sampled case vignettes of publicly accessible 3D printing toolkits.

4.1 Research Approach

The research approach in *Part III* builds upon the findings from *Part II* and addresses the research problem from a different perspective. *Part II* was an exploratory study, and it looked at the research problem from the user's perspective in the user setting. In *Part III* the research approach is narrowed down to explore the solution space of each toolkit and address the research question by taking the toolkit artifact's perspective. The structure of the solution space of toolkits is explored and systematized.

Even if the object of study has shifted from the organizational to the technical, the research question is a "How" question on a contemporary phenomenon on which little is known. Toolkit solution space has been extensively discussed in the context of mass customization and the perspective of the creative process in design. To fulfill the research objective, the study looks at solution space holistically for toolkits of user innovation and design in 3D printing and examines it as a complex system that can be simplified. Since this is a rather new perspective of the phenomenon, it uses an exploratory qualitative method to discover (Eisenhardt, 1989) and generate categories and propositions.

The study aims to investigate systematically and in depth the contemporary state of the art of toolkits in 3D printing. It also addresses a "how" question with little control over events, with many variables of interest and can take advantage of multiple sources of data, hence making case study research suitable for this study. A multiple case study design is chosen, with a single unit of analysis for all the cases (Yin, 2009). A case here refers to a toolkit in 3D printing and the solution space of the toolkit is the unit of analysis. It iteratively analyzed and compared solution space of each toolkit across cases to categorize solution space and identified mechanism found in toolkits for simplifying solution space. The research approach of this study follows the overall research approach of the thesis of moving from the outer environment to the inner structure of the solution space. Figure 15 presents the research approach of *Part III* in the overall context of the thesis. The next section explains the research design followed.

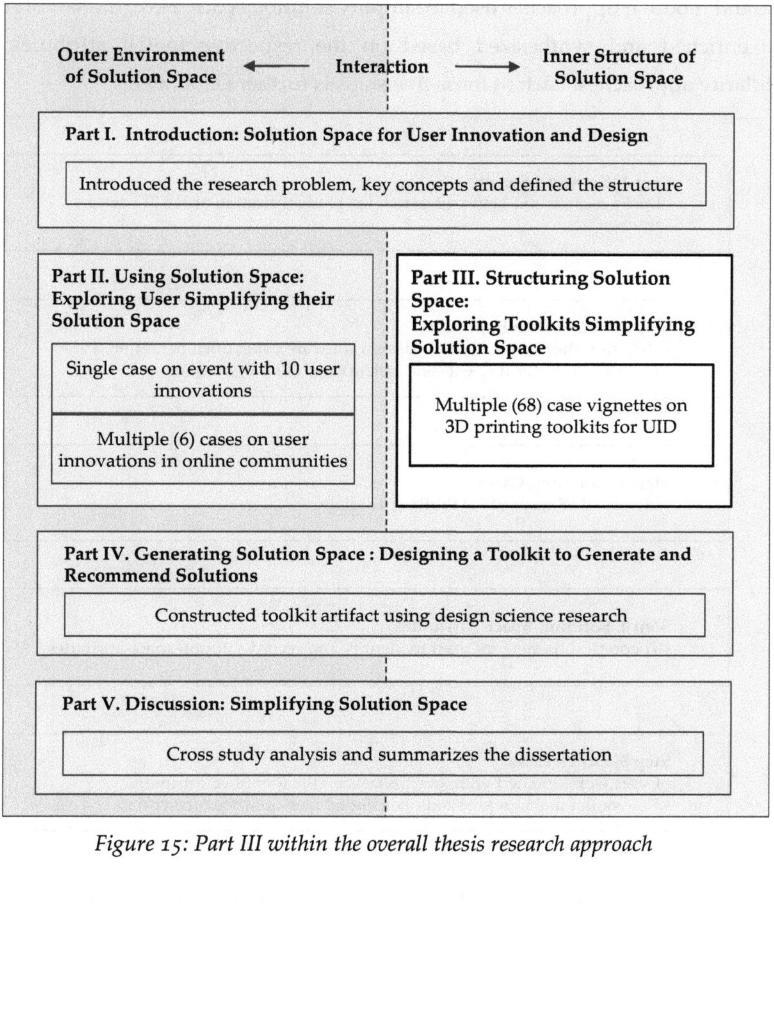

Figure 15: Part III within the overall thesis research approach

4.2 Research Design

The research design of this study has the following five steps. The first step was to conduct a systematic keyword search to identify 3D design software. Second, data regarding the 3D design software was gathered and developed into case vignettes. Third, the 3D design software cases were screened to a sample of 3D printing toolkits based on requirements of toolkits for user innovation and design and access to their solution space. Fourth, data from these toolkits was analyzed along relevant concepts in theory of modularity and design space analysis to derive the attributes of solution space and modular approaches used to simplify solution space. Fifth, the sample cases were enriched and synthesized based on the respective toolkit attributes and modularity approaches. Each of these five steps is further elaborated.

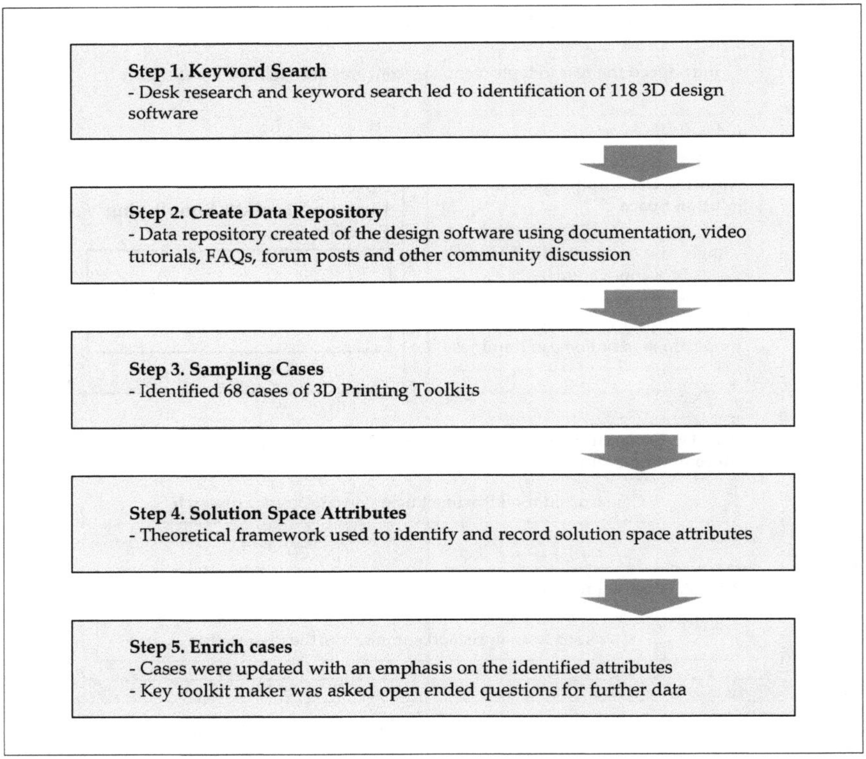

Figure 16: Research design for exploring toolkit solution space

4.2.1 Keyword Search

As the study focusses on toolkits for end users, it was limited to toolkits publicly available to end users and available online in the form of web-based applications, downloadable software for PC or downloadable mobile apps. The first step was to identify relevant software that allowed users to design in 3D. It was done using desk research and keyword search. Direct keyword search for the search terms '3D printing', '3D design' and '3D tools' using Google itself resulted in resulted in 89.3 million, 454 million and 254 million results respectively. Hence, the search results for these terms were limited to the first 100 results for each keyword, and the search was repeated with Bing and Yahoo online searches for new results. Overall, these search approaches identified 118 instances of 3D design software. For each design software, the name, organization behind it, URL and contact email were recorded.

4.2.2 Create Data Repository

The websites of the 3D design software were then examined in the second step, and all relevant data such as documentation, video tutorials, FAQs, support information, forum posts and other community discussion were recorded in a central repository and subsequently used to create the case vignettes. Each case vignette followed a structure that included meta-data of the 3D design software, such as the organization providing it, its availability, and the type of output they generated. The data collected for the vignettes was used for screening the cases in the following step.

4.2.3 Sampling Cases

For the third step, the design software was functionally trialed whenever the full or demo version was freely available, and the software that was not freely accessible were excluded. Some of the 3D printing toolkits were only web forms to get users' preferences, but they did not provide users a direct visualization of the 3D design they were customizing. These were also filtered out keeping in mind that toolkits need to provide users trial and error cycles (von Hippel & Katz, 2002). The 3D design software cases were also screened to see if their outputs could be used for 3D printing. Hence, the requirement was that they generated solid 3D shapes that can be printed (use established formats for 3D printing like .STL or .OBJ) or directly connected to 3D printing services. It filtered out cases of 3D design software that did not create closed 3D shapes (such as3D animation software). CAD systems that were purely for professionals were filtered out as well to yield a sample of 68 cases.

4.2.4 Solution Space Attributes

In the fourth step, the cases were analyzed, using modularity theory and design spaces as a framework. The framework was explained in further detail in the previous section. After multiple iterations of analysis, the attributes of solution space were identified and recorded. The identification of the attributes was conducted in a grounded manner, within the framework dimensions. Mechanisms of modularity used to simplify the complexity of designing in 3D were also documented in the cases.

4.2.5 Enrich cases

In the final step, the identified attributes and modularity mechanisms derived in the previous step were used to code and enrich the cases. The cases were repeatedly updated using data from the repository that pertained to solution space attributes and mechanisms of simplifying solution space based on modularity. Along with the data in the repository, the founders of the toolkit maker Mixee Labs was also interviewed for 45 minutes and asked additional open questions over email to provide additional insights in the special case of 'meta-toolkits.' The interview was recorded and transcribed. The interview transcription and email responses were coded based on the theoretical framework and used to update the cases on Mixee Labs' toolkits.

4.3 Data Sample

The sixty-eight identified toolkits in the data sample were offered to users by both 3D printing services as well as external toolkit makers. The toolkits offered users two ways of 3D printing. Thirty-eight toolkits used APIs (Application Program Interfaces) provided by 3D printing services such as Shapeways, i.materialise, Sculpteo, etc. and directly connected to them. The others allowed users to download or save their 3D designs in the form of standard 3D printing file formats such as STL. A bulk of the sample (45 toolkits) in the sample were linked to 3D printing related organizations such as the services mentioned above and Thingiverse the online 3D printing community from Makerbot. Out of the 68 cases of toolkits for user design in 3D printing, 54 toolkits were web based, and 14 were desktop software available to download and install. Out of the web-based toolkits, 11 allowed users to design online and to download the design files while 43 web-based toolkits restricted user designs to their servers and directly link with 3D printing services. The desktop-based toolkits all allowed users to save their designs and print it themselves. Table 12 lists the sample toolkits used in the study.

Table 12: Sample of 68 toolkits selected for cases on toolkit solution space

3D Tin	Cus. iPhone Case	Meshmixer	Shapeways Minetoys
3D Trophy Factory	Cus. Lithopane	Mixee Knotty Ring	Shapeways Mineways
Adobe Photoshop	Cus. Torus Knot	Mixee Me Figurines	Shapeways Sake Set
Ambretine Koeketine	DAMN Cufflinks	Mixee Round Cufflinks	Shapeways Shapewright
Anne Zeilien Gold	Draw your own earrings	Mixee Square Cuff Links	Sketchup Make
Anne Zeilien Silver	Dreamforge Cookie Caster	Mr. Maria Night Lamps	Sketchup Pro
Archipelis	Electrobloom ring	ODO	Skimlab
Archipelis Custom Ring	Figure Totem	OpenSCAD	Super Flowers
Archipelis Poker Chip	Flower	Parametric Cookie Cutter	Text Totem
Autodesk 123D Catch	Fontbox	Parametric Music Box	The Vibe iPhone case
Autodesk 123D Design	Jweel embossed ring	Parametric Parts	Tinkercad
Autodesk 123D Sculpt +	Jweel Freestyle Pendant	Printcraft	Toyze
Cafe Costume	Jweel Text Pendant	Quark Jewelry	Uformit
Cell Cycle	Jweel Text Ring	Ring Shapewright	Universal Phone Car Mount
CubeTeam	Kees Customizer	Sculptris	Wall Mount Key Holder
Cus. Battery Tray	Materialise Fluid Forms	Sealring	Wave Bracelet
Cus. Easy Gyro	Materialise Fluid Vase	Sertae Knotwork	Zbrush

5 Findings: Simplifying Solution Space for Users

After creating the case database of toolkits and their solution spaces, they were analyzed and categorized. The categorization of the toolkits further enabled the identification of mechanisms for simplifying solution space. This chapter presents the findings of the study. They consist of two sections. The first section provides an analysis of the cases. Modularity-in-use led to the development of a 2x2-matrix framework for categorizing toolkit solution space. The section describes the dimensions and the quadrants of the framework. Analysis of the cases using modularity-in-design follows. Both analyses led to the identification of mechanisms found in these toolkits that simplify solution space for non-expert users. The second section presents these mechanisms in the form of propositions.

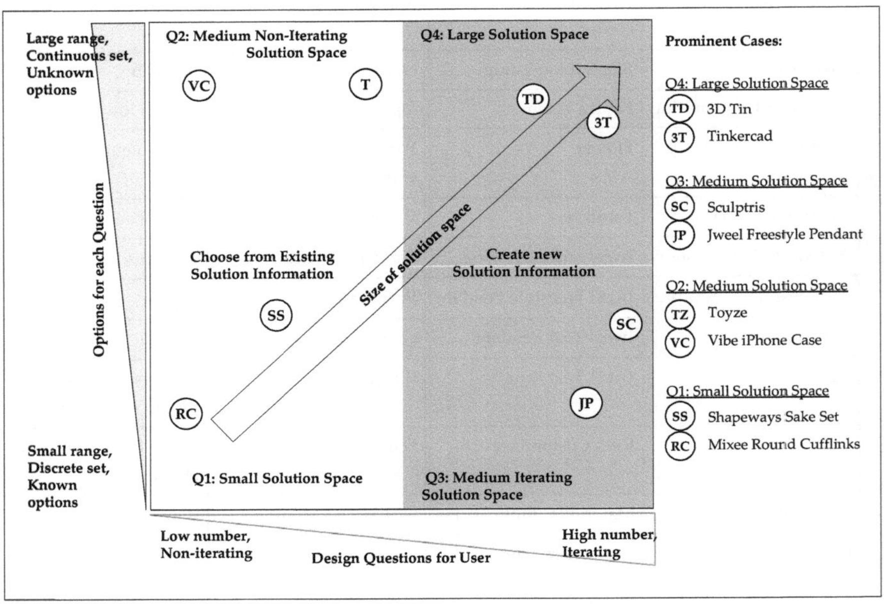

Figure 17: Categorization of solution spaces in 3D printing toolkits

5.1 Analysis of Toolkit Solution Space

The solution spaces of the 68 toolkits were analyzed using the two modularity principles described previously. First, as users follow the modularity-in-use principle to design their products, toolkits solutions space was categorized based on the number of design questions and their respective number of design options (see Figure 17). Section 5.1.1, describes the four categories, with the help of exemplary toolkits. Section 5.1.2 describes the analysis of toolkit solution space based on their resulting modularity-in-design.

5.1.1 Solution Space Categorization based on Modularity-in-use

The solution space categorization uses the framework of modularity-in-use and is in the form of a 2x2-matrix. The horizontal axis consisting of the number of design questions a user will answer when designing with the toolkit. The vertical axis of the matrix represents design options for the design questions in the toolkit solution space. The solution space of a toolkit can be placed against each of these axis based on the nature of the typical design questions and design options a user will have to address when using the toolkit.

5.1.1.1 Horizontal Axis: Design Questions

The horizontal axis consists of design questions that can range from low to high in number. Usually, design questions in a toolkit with a small solution space are typically a *fixed set* and *low in number*. The toolkit for configuring cufflinks in Chapter 3 is an example with seven design questions (material, color, etching, etc.). Users can answer these questions in any order and often have default values set if the user does not answer any of them. There can be more design questions in more complicated configurators, but they remain fixed, with each question representing one fixed level of decision making by the user.

It is in contrast with toolkits with large solution spaces used for developing new solution information, where along with many design questions, the questions are answered *iteratively* by the user to build new designs that are more complex. Each design question is a function or an operation of the toolkit, like drawing a cube or drawing a sphere and these questions are repeated many times to build a 3D design. The order of the design questions may also be necessary if they involve irreversible operations (e.g. deleting a part of the design). Non-expert users when using such toolkits need to go through many learning by doing cycles, exploring these functions and their combinations before they can start effectively.

Table 13: The two axis of solution space categorization

Axis	Low Level of Axis	High Level of Axis
Design Questions	• Non-iterating questions • Less number of questions	• Iterating questions • Many basis questions
Design Options	• Discrete set of options • Small range of variation • Known to the user	• Continuous set • Large range of variation • Unknown to the user

5.1.1.2 Vertical Axis: Design Options

The vertical axis consists of design options for the design questions explained above. While the range of the number of design options is the most obvious indicator of the size of the solution space, it is not sufficient and often cannot be measured in the case of many design questions. Hence, three ways of categorizing design options w.r.t the size of toolkit solution space were altogether identified. Firstly, if there are a *discrete set* of design options, then the range can vary between small and large. An example of this would be a design question that is answered by selecting from a drop-down menu or a checklist. Secondly, the design options can be differentiated between being a discrete set (dropdown, checklist, etc.) or a continuous set of options. A *continuous set* of options can be in the form of a slider between two values or a text box that accepts any string, where a user can potentially have close to infinite options, even if the options are bounded by some limits. Thirdly, the solution space can have options that are *known* or *unknown* to the user. Known options are those the user is familiar with, thereby the selection can be visualized by the user, and it requires lower user involvement to start designing. The cufflinks configurator in Chapter 3 has little icons that allow users to preview each of the different materials that can be chosen. Cufflinks printed in a particular material is also easy to visualize, as users would have likely handled the material in the past. On the other hand, unknown options need to be first explored by the user in learning-by-doing cycles before selecting one. So these are considered to increase solution space for the user. Hence, design options can be classified and ordered by comparing them using these three forms.

The two axes form the 2X2 matrix categorizing solution space of toolkits. The four quadrants do not have precise boundaries but provide a good understanding of solution space of 3D printing toolkits. It can be used to analyze and compare both toolkits for existing solution information as well as for new solution information. The quadrants of the solution spaces are explained in the following sections using a few exemplary cases of toolkits. The quadrants are named regarding increasing solution space (roughly) and described in that order.

5.1.1.3 Quadrant Q1: Small Solution Space

The quadrant Q1 of the matrix represents a small solution space and has the simplest toolkits. They tend to have a discrete small set of fixed questions with a small set of fixed design options for each question. The *Mixee Square Cufflinks* is a simple configurator that falls in this quadrant. It allows users to select different materials and finishing for cufflinks and enter initials on them. Hence, the design questions are of the form *"What ring material do I use?"* and *"What initials (text) do I use?"* each of which has a limited number of design options. The questions and options are relatively known; hence, they require much lesser user involvement. A screenshot of the square cufflinks toolkit is presented in Figure 18. The *Sake Set Creator (K)* described earlier is similar as it allows users to change the shape of a Sake pot along certain dimensions and configure the pattern. The solution space offered here typically leads to a limited number of possible solutions. They may not be perfect solutions, but for the average user with a high cost of user involvement and lower aspirational levels, these solutions are sufficient. Design questions in this quadrant were often also posed to the user one after the other, in a fixed order to make it further easier for the user.

Figure 18: Screenshot of square cufflinks from Mixee Labs[19]

5.1.1.4 Quadrant Q2: Medium Non-Iterating Solution Space

Quadrant Q2 represents a medium solution space, where there are a fixed and relatively low number of design questions, but users have a broad range of unlimited design options that can be explored by users. The *Vibe iPhone Case Creator* (VC) is an example toolkit that falls within this quadrant. It etches the waveform of an audio clip onto an iPhone case. This toolkit has only one major design question for the user, *"What sound clip should I use?"* However, for this design question, any audio clip is a possible design option as long as it can be uploaded onto Soundcloud, an audio sharing service. Hence, the user has bounded, but infinite number of design options. The bounds or limits to the solution space in this case are much broader than the limits for the cufflinks configurator seen previously. While a user would mostly know the

[19] https://www.mixeelabs.com/creator/square-cufflinks Screenshot retrieved on 01.12.2015

audio clip the user wants, the user may still need to try out many possible options of audio clips, to check the visual aesthetics of the generated design, leading to many learning-by-doing cycles. Figure 19 explains the design process using The Vibe. *Toyze* (TZ) is another toolkit that falls within this quadrant. It is a 3D printing toolkit where users can create, customize, and order figurines of popular mobile game characters in various poses, outfits, and accessories. The design questions in this toolkit are again limited and fixed. However, each design question has a significant number of design options, which are often new to the user. The user needs to first be familiarized with these options through many trial and error cycles before selecting an option for the design question.

Figure 19: Screenshot of The Vibe, a toolkit to design custom iPhone cases [20]

5.1.1.5 Quadrant Q3: Medium Iterating Solution Space

The other quadrant of medium solution space is Q3. In this quadrant, the solution space offers is in the form of a vast number of iterating design questions, which have

[20] http://www.shapeways.com/creator/thevibe Screenshot retrieved on 15.05.2012

relatively fewer design options. These design questions arise when a user uses a function and the user will have to use these functions repeatedly to develop a design. Each of these questions has a limited set of simple, easy to visualize design options. The toolkit *Sculptris* (SC) is a toolkit that exemplifies this quadrant. Using Sculptris, users can design in 3D as if they were sculpting with clay. It offers sculpting functions such as smooth, sharp, flatten, grab etc. users can apply at various degrees of intensity, and to particular areas of the 3D design, just like a sculptor would operate with real clay. Hence, the questions are *"which sculpting tool do I use?" "How strongly should the tool be applied?", "Where should the tool be applied"* etc. The base set of these design questions is small and easy to comprehend and the design options for these questions are limited. However, despite the simplicity in design questions and options, these sculpting tools can on repeated application, design very complex shapes. Figure 20 is a screenshot of Sculptris used for designing a 3D model from iterating design functions. The *Jweel Freestyle Pendant* (JP) is another toolkit that has a very similar solution space. It has a smaller solution space than Sculptris by reducing the design questions and options even further for users to focus on designing finer jewelry items.

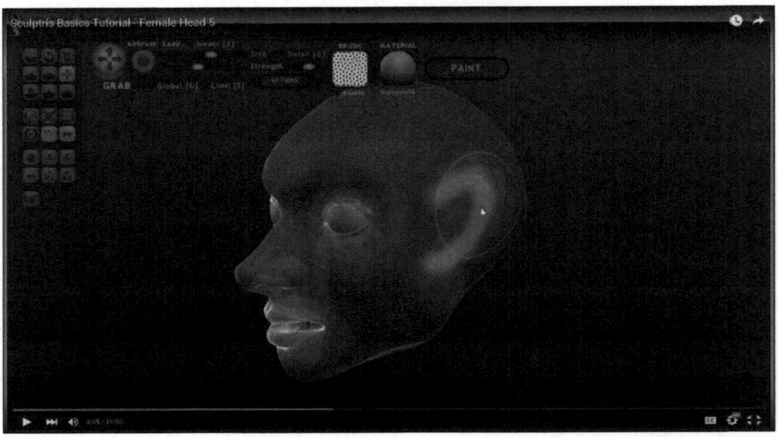

Figure 20: Screenshot of tutorial of Sculptris displaying its design capabilities

5.1.1.6 Quadrant Q4: Large Solution Space

Quadrant Q4 consists of large toolkit solution spaces that require a lot of user involvement. The solution space here consists of a vast number of design questions, which are iterating from a larger basic set of functions. Each of the design questions also has a continuous set of design options for the user to select. Often these design questions and options need to be trialed in learning-by-doing cycles before the user gets familiar and can start using the solution space. The 3D printing toolkits *Tinkercad* (TD) and *3D Tin* (3T) fall in this quadrant. They are web based 3D design tools dedicated to 3D printing, which give users a lot of flexibility but are much less complex than professionally used CAD software. These toolkits provide users many basic 3D shapes such as cubes, spheres, cylinders, etc. to use as building blocks to design. Users can configure the dimensions of these components, then place them in different positions and add to or subtract from existing shapes. Hence the user asks design questions such as *"What shape do I use?", "How is the shape configured?", "Where is the shape placed?", "Does the shape add or subtract to other shapes"* etc. repeatedly in many iterations to design complex 3D shapes. Figure 21 exhibits a 3D design created by users with Tinkercad.

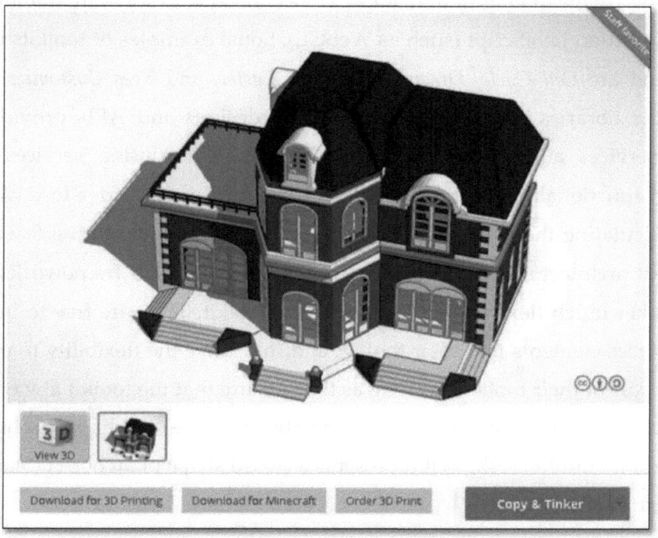

Figure 21: Screenshot of a user design created with Tinkercad

5.1.2 Solution Space and Modularity-in-design

The categorization of solution space by design questions and design options, which together represent modularity-in-use, resulted in the matrix discussed above. The other form of modularity that is used as a lens to study simplification of solution space is *modularity-in-design*. Users use solution space of a toolkit to design their products, but they do not do it alone. There is modularity-in-design involved in products developed by users with these toolkits, which was analyzed and is presented. In the sample of 68 toolkits used in this case study, while product design when using a toolkit is expected to come from the user and manufacturer, there is additional design modularity seen in 48 of these toolkits. Product design in these cases may have additional contributors, such as toolkit makers, users who design (both novices and experts), users with their 3D printers, or organizations providing a 3D printing service. The modularity in design is further explained by looking at the architecture of the toolkits that reveal design rules between the modules.

5.1.2.1 Toolkits developed from Scratch

Thirty-two of the toolkits in the sample were created with software frameworks and libraries based on JavaScript (such as WebGL). Some examples of toolkits created by this method are *Cell Cycle, Dreamforge Cookie Caster,* and *Kees Customizer*. In these toolkits, the libraries are used to visualize 3D designs and APIs provided by 3D printing services augment them. The API from 3D printing services rendered additional functionalities in the toolkit such as sending an order to a 3D printing service, calculating the printing cost, checking the design for printing feasibility, etc. This toolkit architecture of using programming libraries and frameworks gives the toolkit maker much flexibility in designing the toolkit. They are free to include any user interfaces elements into their toolkit, and they have the flexibility to use any 3D shapes as part of their toolkits, as long as they ensure that the toolkit always creates a design that is 3D printable. For a 3D design to be printable, the shape is required to be a watertight manifold mesh, so it represents a closed shape of an object (Stava, Vanek, Benes, Carr, & Měch, 2012).

The toolkit maker thus creates a 3D design that acts as the foundation of the toolkit and then identifies certain aspects of it that can be considered customizable. These aspects are parameterized so that users are free to change them and customize this 3D design. The toolkit architecture results in a fixed and small number of design questions and associated options, making it ideal to create unique and innovative basic toolkits. However, the toolkit maker who does the bulk of the design needs an advanced knowledge of browser based programming languages and libraries used for 3D rendering. The toolkit maker has much freedom and does not follow specific design rules (Baldwin & Clark, 2001). Hence, this method needs some interaction between the toolkit maker and the 3D printing service, where the service evaluates the toolkits before verifying and accepting them.

5.1.2.2 Toolkits Developed by Users

The second group consisted of 16 basic toolkits users developed themselves, using intermediate systems provided to them. These systems acted as meta-toolkits that enabled these users to create basic toolkits. The first meta-toolkit identified is the *Customizer* app by Thingiverse. Users create scripts written in OpenSCAD that describes a 3D design of an object. Users can parameterize this design, specify limits for each parameter, and include appropriate user interface elements such as drop-down boxes, sliders, checkboxes, radio buttons, etc. They can then upload these scripts into the Customizer App, which converts the scripts to basic toolkits called 'Customizables.'

The *Mixee Creator* is also a meta-toolkit that imports scripts by users written in 'Three.js,' a powerful JavaScript library for 3D designs that is based on WebGL. Similar to the OpenSCAD method used by the Customizer App, the Mixee creators also provides a library of shapes and geometries, which users can use to create a 3D object with parameters. The platform promises to add further advanced geometries as requested. An example Creator is the *Mixee Ring Customizer (M),* where users can create customizable rings with text on them.

Tinkercad, the toolkit mentioned earlier also uses this approach by letting users develop their parameterized shapes using JavaScript based libraries and uploading them to their servers. Users can use these parametric shapes as starting points or building blocks for their designs. *Digital formation* takes this principle further through *Odo*, their Software as a Service offering to designers. It enables designers to build customization toolkits rapidly that are already integrated with 3D printing services and e-commerce websites.

In summary, these meta-toolkits allow users to create their own toolkits by allowing them to integrate user input elements (such as dropdowns, radio buttons, sliders, etc.) and a library of 3D geometric shapes (such as a cube, sphere, torus, cylinder, etc.). These elements are integrated using various operations (such as move, scale and merge these shapes). The meta-toolkits offer an easy to understand set of design questions for the user. Firstly, *what are the underlying shapes of the user's design?* Secondly, *where are these shapes located?* Thirdly, *which parameters of these shapes are customizable?* The user asks these questions iteratively to have sufficient design freedom while still being relatively less complex when compared to programming toolkits from scratch. The meta-toolkits create customizable designs based on embedded 3D printing related design rules, with a simplified solution space that users define.

The categorization of solution space based on design questions and options and mechanisms of modularity used to share design contributions between entities lead to the identification of mechanisms to simplify toolkit solution space. The next section presents these mechanisms.

5.2 Mechanisms for Simplifying Solution Space

To identify how solution space of toolkits in 3D printing can be simplified, four mechanisms were established in the 68 compiled cases of toolkits that gave users flexibility in design while reducing their involvement or encouraging their participation in the design process. These four mechanisms are described below, and propositions are made. Figure 22 illustrates the four mechanisms using the categorization framework developed earlier.

Design questions with a wide range of options that are unknown to users require many cycles of trial and error before users become familiar and can start using a toolkit. Breaking these design questions down into design questions whose outcomes users already know encourages their involvement. Sculptris and Jweel Freestyle Pendant, the two cases explained in the earlier categorization can be used to design a wide variety of 3D shapes without prior knowledge using simple sculpting functions. It reduces design options in the solution space (Q4 to Q3 in Figure 22) at the cost of going through more but known design questions. It leads us to the following proposition:

Proposition 1: *Offering known, iterative design questions and options instead of unknown design questions and options can simplify solution space for users.*

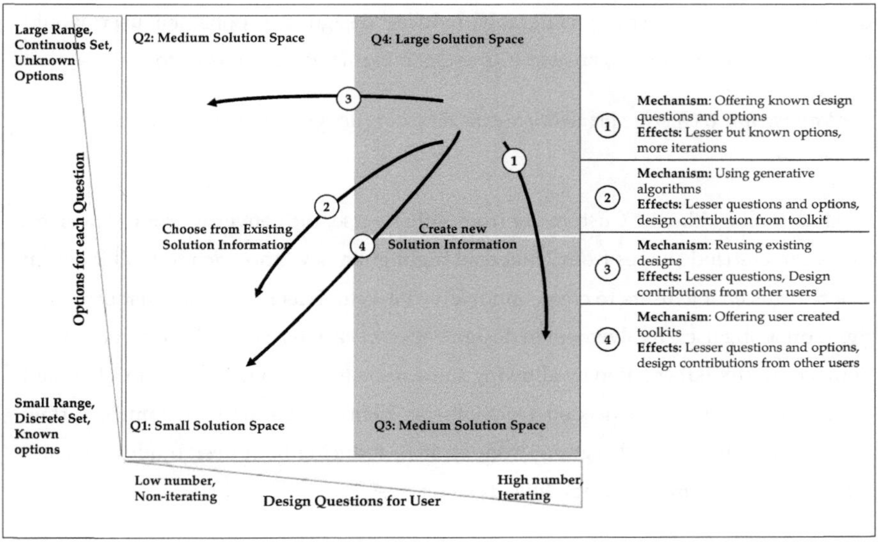

Figure 22: Mechanisms for simplifying solution space for users in 3D printing.

Toolkits like *Cell Cycle* and *Super Flowers* customizable generate their 3D designs by algorithms. The generated designs are inspired by nature such as microscopic biological cells and flower petals with parameters that users can customize. The users do not have to design complicated shapes as algorithms do the design work, thus reducing design questions and options for the user. This also ensures that the solution space has variety in design output while being within the aesthetic limits set by the toolkit makers. Hence also potentially eliminating certain design options from the solution space (Q4 to Q1 in Figure 22). This leads us to:

> ***Proposition 2:*** *Using algorithms to generate 3D design can simplify toolkit solution space for users*

The *Autodesk 123D Catch* generates 3D designs from user-uploaded photos. The *Fluid Form* toolkits connect to external services like Google Maps and Google Earth and generate 3D designs from maps or 3D images of these locations. Tinkercad, Sketchup, 3D Tin, etc. connect to a design database where users can access designs from other users and improve them. These features reduce a lot of the design effort of users and hence simplify toolkit solution space by reducing their contribution to design. This mechanism considerably reduces design questions the user would otherwise have required to answer (Q4 to Q2 in Figure 22). It leads us to:

> ***Proposition 3:*** *Offering the ability to extend existing designs can simplify solution space for users.*

Meta-toolkits like the Customizer from Thingiverse, the converter from Mixeelabs, the parameterized shapes from Tinkercad highlight a new approach to toolkit design where firms enable users to create innovative basic toolkits rather than just products, thus spreading user involvement in design between various users. These meta-toolkits democratize toolkit creation by allowing some users to design toolkits themselves and reduce the contribution needed from others. Hence, users only customize certain parameters rather than designing from scratch, reducing both design questions and options (Q4 to Q1 in Figure 22). It leads us to:

> ***Proposition 4:*** *Offering users the ability to create their own toolkits can simplify solution space for some users.*

6 Discussion

Part III of the dissertation is a comprehensive study on toolkits in 3D printing, it adds to research on toolkits for user innovation and design and modularity theory, by providing a categorization for solution space that encompasses both basic and expert toolkits and identifying mechanisms with which modularity simplifies solution space for users. This chapter discusses the theoretical contributions and findings, compares them with existing research, and describes the limitations of the study.

The key research contribution this study brings is further depth in the concept of toolkit solution space, and it looks at how it is structured and simplified for the non-expert user. In doing so, it identifies and describes interesting mechanisms in the field of 3D printing that simplify solution space which may be extended to other problem domains such as do-it-yourself electronics (Baafi & Millner, 2011; Cvijikj & Michahelles, 2011; Mikhak, Lyon, & Gorton, 2003), app development, etc. The resulting modularity based framework can be used as a theory to analyze solution space, and the developed propositions can be used as a theory to predict solution space design and construct toolkit artifacts based on the identified mechanisms (Gregor, 2006). User created toolkits corroborate with the study on toolkits used in the game 'The Sims' where expert users, discontent with the official toolkits provided by the manufacturer, created and used their own toolkits that also had a high demand among other users.

The approach of offering meta-toolkits extends the 'sticky information' approach of von Hippel (von Hippel, 1994; von Hippel & Katz, 2002). Instead of just transferring sticky knowledge from firms to users, it extends the purpose of toolkits. Toolkits first select appropriate sticky knowledge relevant to a particular user group and then transfer it to the users. This multi-level approach has implications on how users, user communities, and firms can truly leverage each other's capabilities to develop more innovative and differentiated products. The role of the manufacturer in design inputs is quite limited to the meta-toolkit offered to its users. The next level of design inputs comes from expert users who use this meta-toolkit and create innovative designs and define what attributes of the designs can be customized. Other users provide final design inputs by creating their customized and innovative products.

Out of the four mechanisms identified, the first encourages non-expert users to use a toolkit by making each design decision easy. However, expert users may find it frustrating, as they will have to perform many iterations of these design decisions. The other three mechanisms reduce design questions and options for the user. Similar mechanisms can be seen in other contexts. Using algorithms to filter design questions and options can be seen in recommender systems for decision making (De Bruyn, Liechty, Huizingh, & Lilien, 2008). Design tools that learn and acquire problem specific knowledge and then support decision making have been developed and presented (Gero, 1996). Likewise, sharing existing designs is a common mechanism that has been reported in toolkits for mobile (Piller et al., 2004) and computer (L. B. Jeppesen, 2005; Prügl & Schreier, 2006) games. However, the conversion mechanism by which existing non-3D design content such as photos, external services, etc. can be converted to 3D designs can be considered novel to this field. Furthermore, 3D printing toolkits seem to take two approaches regarding openness. One approach is through a cloud-based service, they restrict all creation to the toolkit servers, hence restricting design sharing while encouraging the selling of designs to other users. The other approach is to offer a toolkit that allows users to save their designs and share them or to connect to open design databases.

6.1 Meta-toolkit for User Created Toolkits

The study highlights the meta-toolkit as it improves upon the traditional approach of creating solution space of basic toolkits in 3D printing. It involves creating toolkits in-house or by professional designers, as one would develop regular web apps. The toolkit has a 3D visualization component created by web-based programming languages and libraries for rendering objects in 3D. The toolkit creator decides the solution space, and it consists of parameters for users to customize. On the other hand, offering a meta-toolkit enables users to create their solution space for toolkits. The meta-toolkit is a system dedicated to creating basic toolkits in 3D printing. It uses base elements and operations that are 3D printable to enable users (Helminen et al., 2015) and can be considered closer to the overall aim of democratizing innovation (von Hippel, 2005) that was found wanting (Goduscheit & Jørgensen, 2013).

The meta-toolkit thus enables users the flexibility to innovate through 3D printable designs by repeatedly answering a smaller set of design questions. It contrasts with using all-purpose 3D design software libraries. From this meta-toolkit, expert users can create basic toolkits with small solution spaces of a fixed number of design questions aimed at non-expert users. Figure 3.presents a model of the meta-toolkit. Hence, this *toolkit for user created toolkits* forms a new approach ideal for simplifying solution space of 3D printing, where design flexibility and user involvement goes hand in hand.

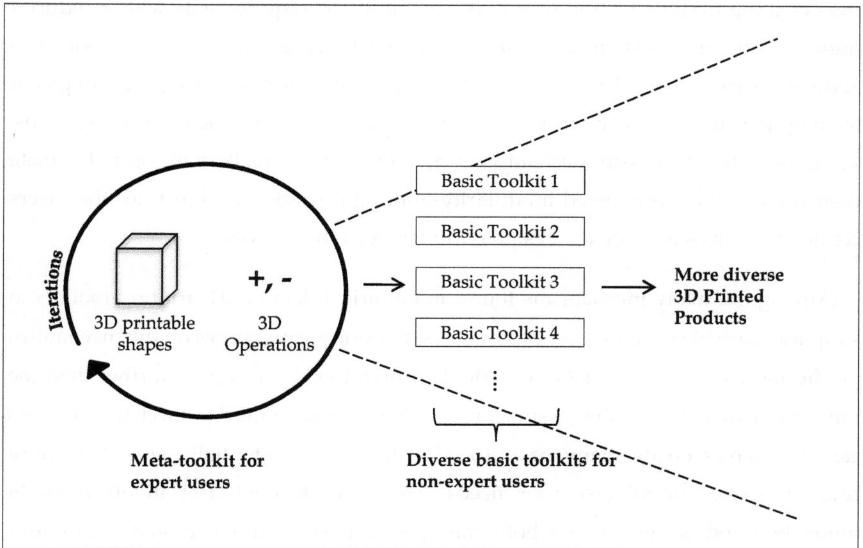

Figure 23: Meta-toolkit' for user designed toolkits

6.2 Conclusion

To conclude, this study explains how toolkits in 3D printing structure and simplify the potentially significant solution space in 3D designs for the non-expert user. It improves on existing categorization of toolkits between expert (high-end) and basic (low-end) toolkits by providing identifiable and measurable attributes of 3D design solution space in terms of established theory of modularity and design space analysis. Future studies on solution space structuring can use this categorization as a foundation.

The empirical cases analyzed with the perspective of modularity revealed four mechanisms in toolkits for 3D printing that simplified solution space for non-expert users. The first mechanism encourages non-expert users to use the toolkit by making each design decision (question and its associated options) easy, thus reducing the learning curve. The other three mechanisms reduce design questions and options for the user. The second mechanism is using algorithms that generate designs for the user thus creating designs for the user that meet aesthetic requirements with a reduced number of design questions and options. The third mechanism found in toolkits is to allow users to extend existing designs. It can be in the form of sharing 3D designs or fetching part of the design information from external services such as photos, maps, 3D games, etc. The fourth mechanism is by offering meta-toolkits for users to create their own toolkits. It allowed modularity-in-design by strict design rules that users create themselves to share the design effort between themselves.

Among the many mechanisms found in empirical data of 3D printing toolkits to simplify solution space for non-expert users, the study emphasizes on the mechanism of offering users meta-toolkits to create their own toolkits as it goes further than the other mechanisms regarding democratizing innovation. With this mechanism, users can themselves create many basic toolkits that could potentially span the entire solution space and diverse user needs. This multi-layered user involvement in innovation and design bridges both concepts of innovation and customization and effectively handles the problem of structuring toolkit solution space.

Part IV

Generating Solution Space:

Designing a Toolkit to Generate and Recommend Solutions

1 Needs and Objectives

The previous Parts of the dissertation have established the following points: Users of products have heterogeneous needs that are unmet by standardized production. New technologies have the potential to provide a large solution space with which users can innovate and design based on their distinctive needs, but this solution space needs to be simplified for the non-expert user. This simplification is done from the user's end by initially using toolkits with minimum solution space needed and reusing existing design in the form of off-the-shelf products. It is also done within the toolkit itself, by different mechanisms for reusing design and by leveraging known design questions and options and by reducing design questions and options for the user. *Part IV* follows the previous parts with a study that extends these learnings from the past two studies.

Mass customization literature has extensively researched development of solution space for non-expert users, which mirrors the problems with developing solution space discussed earlier. Users have been shown to enjoy the process of self-design when using toolkits that allow them to design freely and exhibit the "I designed it myself" effect (Franke et al., 2010). However, also a mass-confusion effect can arise due to overloading the user with a wide range of configuration and design steps (Huffman & Kahn, 1998; Teresko, 1994) or in other words, navigate through a large solution space. This problem has been called the product variety paradox in sales configurators (Salvador & Forza, 2004).

It can be worse when users do not explicitly know their needs but have implicit needs, which surface only as users try out the toolkit (von Hippel & von Krogh, 2013). They go through various trial and error processes of designing and evaluating their products until they stumble upon products that meet their needs. While initially intriguing, this process can quickly become frustrating when each cycle of design and evaluation takes time. As users design their products with toolkits, it is assumed that they have clearly defined needs and after a few learning-by-doing cycles, they can break down the steps required to design their products. However, beyond simple configurators, users have to go through a large number of design questions and options that require them to be very involved with the toolkit and become very familiar with its design question and options.

Toolkits that provide users with *focused navigation,* i.e., equip users to arrive quickly at required solutions have been suggested for configurators as a way to reduce the product variety paradox (Trentin, Perin, & Forza, 2013). However, providing focused navigation to toolkits for user innovation and design is a challenge, especially with the inherent contradiction of design flexibility and user involvement that this dissertation has repeatedly mentioned. It is typically characterized by unstable requirements and constraints that are based on ill-defined environmental contexts (Rittel & Webber, 1984). Due to the nature of this challenge, any solution would require complex interactions between the solution and sub-components of the problem. A toolkit for user innovation and design with focused navigation would be critically dependent on human cognitive abilities to produce effective solutions and can potentially draw upon human social abilities to produce effective solutions. These characteristics of the challenge qualify it to be a wicked problem and an ideal candidate to be solved by the new design (Hevner, March, Park, & Ram, 2004; Peffers & Tuunanen, 2007). This study hence addresses the research question:

RQ3: Can a toolkit that generates recommendations simplify solution space and enable non-expert users?

The objectives of the study are to design, implement, and evaluate a toolkit prototype that provides focused navigation to non-expert users while addressing their implicit needs using the Design Science Research (DSR) method. The toolkit prototype generates new solution information in the form of completed solutions and recommends these solutions to users. It also focusses navigation for the user by aiming to reduce the number of interactions needed for the user to find the solution.

Designing *storage cabinets* was chosen as the context for the toolkit prototype as designing them required a sufficiently large solution space, but at the same time, the artifacts and results generated were easy to comprehend and can be generalized to other scenarios. The toolkit is a web-based system that generates finished designs of cabinets based on explicit needs entered by the user as well as feedback of the user's preferred recommendation. The prototype itself consists of three artifacts: A web-based toolkit interface to the user, an ontology for mapping explicit user needs to product design characteristics, and an algorithm to traverse through the solution space and categorize solutions based on how similar they are to the user.

The toolkit iteratively generates a set of solution recommendations to users. The user selects a finished solution closest to the user's needs rather than designing the solution. Each set of solutions follows from the user's selected solution from the previous set, which is closest to the user's needs. As user gives feedback on each generated set of final solutions, the toolkit uses the feedback to understand the user's implicit needs and to generate the next round of solutions for the user. This toolkit generates solutions that match with the problem (need) information of the user.

The toolkit prototype first designs all possible solution variations based on explicit needs provided by the user. Then through iterative user interactions with sampled sets of solutions, it takes the user to the solutions they need. Doing so provides two benefits. Firstly, the toolkit recognizes implicit needs of the user from every selection made by the user, of the solution closest to their needs and captured. Secondly, it automates tedious design steps needed to arrive at the final product thereby letting the user go through a much more focused navigation in finding a solution when compared to traditional toolkits.

The toolkit was evaluated throughout the design process by observational studies conducted on users. After the first prototype had been built, three experiments were conducted with 40 users, to compare focused navigation between the prototype toolkit and a traditional toolkit used to design storage cabinets. The evaluation studies suggested that this new toolkit design indeed provided a more focused navigation to the user with non-specific preferences.

The designed toolkit prototype has significant research contributions in the organization of user innovation and design. The study extends the problem of focused navigation from configurators to user design toolkits. The toolkit has categorized the solution space based on a ranking of the user's explicit needs. Finally, the design takes the known solution of recommender systems and derives a variant for toolkits for user innovation and design. It thereby follows an exaptation approach of design, taking a known solution for a new problem (Gregor & Hevner, 2013).

The rest of *Part IV* is organized as follows. Chapter 2 of this part provides further literature background and theoretical underpinning needed for design science research. Chapter 3 describes the design science research method used in this study and the environmental context in which it was conducted. Chapter 4 and Chapter 5 present the results of the study, which are in the form of description of the artifacts and the evaluation results respectively. Finally, Chapter 6 concludes the study by summarizing the results and discussing the contributions and implications.

2 Theoretical Foundations for Design

The literature on toolkits for user innovation and design along with the theory on modularity that forms the basis of this study have already been described in the previous parts of this thesis. This chapter will give some additional background on literature required to understand how to develop a toolkit for non-expert users that can generate and recommend solutions to users. It first starts with an overview of *implicit and explicit needs*, which leads to the concept of *need solution pairs*. It is followed by literature related to *mass confusion, decision-making* and *focused navigation* in the context of mass customization toolkits. While toolkits for user innovation and design are not limited to mass customization toolkits, previous literature on design decisions in mass customization toolkits provide useful understanding for this study. Finally, it will provide an overview of appropriate *recommender systems*, which is the technical foundation for the construction of the artifacts in this study. These concepts are relevant to this study as they form the underlying theory needed to develop the toolkit prototype.

2.1 Need solution Pairs

Problem-solving research has traditionally assumed a sequential process of identifying a need, formulating it, and then searching for an optimal solution to the problem. It is similar to the typical design process for constructing artifacts that are followed as a research method for this study as well (Peffers & Tuunanen, 2007). Another approach to problem-solving involves first proposing solutions and identifying any needs they trigger. In these cases, the problem identification comes after discovering a solution. Hence, there is a need landscape and a solution landscape that are connected by need-solution pairs (von Hippel & von Krogh, 2013). In design science research, developing a fitness landscape so that different evolutions of a design can be evaluated instead of evaluating just one design is a similar approach (Gill & Hevner, 2013).

One way of identifying various need-solution pairs is to formulate broad and flexible problems purposefully. These approaches are used in lead user studies (von Hippel, 1986) where the focus is to identify need-solution pairs that may or may not fit (perhaps after some modification) the need-solution landscape of the firm. The positive deviant study approach also uses a similar technique of first identifying existing solutions that meet some people's needs and then checking if they fulfill other people's needs (Krumholz, Curry, & Bradley, 2011).

Using algorithmic searches to find solutions to problems is another way to find need-solution pairs, which is suitable when the problem is well structured. Problem formulators can convert ill-structured problems into well-structured problems (Simon, 1973). The theoretical background of modularity in the previous studies and the involvement of users provide some structure to this otherwise ill-structured problem. The study uses it as a foundational structure that can lead to a partial algorithmic solution.

2.2 Making Design Decisions

When customers are exposed to excessive choice and product related information, they can easily get overwhelmed, confused and frustrated, resulting in sub-optimal decision making (Huffman & Kahn, 1998; Mitchell & Papavassiliou, 1999). Mass-customization toolkits can lead to mass confusion when users need to be more involved in the purchasing process and deal with a large number of design questions and options. Increasing product variations and options turn the positive effect of variety into negative as the complexity increases (Teresko, 1994). Different types of consumer confusion arise with configuration overload. It can happen when a consumer's perception of a configuration task is that 1) it's too complex, 2) the options are not clear, 3) the options are too unsettling, or 4) the options are too similar to be differentiated (Matzler, Waiguny, & Füller, 2007).

Non-expert users, as was earlier defined have no specific knowledge and cannot understand all the aspects of the product. Keeping in mind the perspective of satisficing, non-expert users have a low threshold of which design question or option is 'good enough' when making decisions. Classical theories in social sciences have often assumed rational choice in making decisions, where an individual has personal preferences and acts according to these preferences to maximize his or her personal profit (Scott, 2000). However rational choice theory assumes that individuals have all or most of the relevant knowledge that are required, a stable and well-organized system of preference and the capability to calculate the best option for the individual's purpose based on the knowledge and preferences (Simon, 1955). However, an individual, in reality, has incomplete knowledge and limited decision-making skills that often lead to imperfect decisions (Simon, 1955, 1956). This perspective is critical when designing an artifact for non-expert users.

The other behavioral limitation of individuals is that their preferences are often not inherent but constructed through interactions (Slovic, 1995). They build their preferences through a configuration process, influenced by their incomplete perception of their environment. These preferences are also not stable and can change during the process (Bettman, Luce, & Payne, 1998).

2.3 Focused Navigation in Toolkits

The literature on mass customization toolkits provides some starting points on different interfaces for different types of users. Expert users are very familiar with the product, and they would like to make design decisions directly. On the other hand, non-expert users need support in making design decisions and are more concerned with their needs rather than the specific design decisions. They would prefer an interface where they can express their needs rather than directly modify the design attributes (Huffman & Kahn, 1998).

For configurators, five core capabilities solve the paradox of offering the right solution space. These are flexible navigation, focused navigation, benefit-cost communication, easy comparison functionality and user-friendly product space description (Trentin et al., 2013). Out of these, this study addresses the capability of focused navigation d in this part as a means to simplify solution space for the non-expert user. Focused navigation is the ability to focus a user's search quickly in the solution space on finding the best match to the user's needs (Trentin et al., 2013). The toolkit achieves this by reducing the size of the solution space. Users then have much lesser information to process when making their decisions and can spend a longer time in absorbing this information, building up their preferences and thus make better decisions (Bettman et al., 1998; Syam, Krishnamurthy, & Hess, 2008). An approach that can result in focused navigation is option ranking, where users can order the configurable options by their importance. As the user makes a choice, the solution space gets reduced for the further sub-choices in the solution space (Salvador et al., 2009). Another choice is to have starting points close to the customer's ideal solution. It will decrease the number design decisions that need to be taken to arrive at the solution (Randall et al., 2005).

2.4 Recommender Systems

The design of the toolkit aims at assisting users as they answer each design question and as it follows the approach of DSR, it needs to be based on proven technologies to establish research rigor. Use of recommender systems (RS) is an established technology and technique for providing users with suggestions of products that fulfills customer needs within a greater space of potential products. It provides users suggestions of different items to assist in their decision-making process (Resnick & Varian, 1997). It tries to predict items that match preferences of users and thereby support them when they do not have sufficient knowledge and experience required to evaluate a large variety of choices (Resnick & Varian, 1997). The next few paragraphs explore RS further as it can enable users to simplify solution space by reducing design questions and options.

RS have a broad application area, and they are currently in use in many internet firms' offerings. Amazon, YouTube, Netflix, etc. use them to suggest certain products or content from a large pool of users that they may also like based on their historical preferences. The actual role of RS within an information system, the underlying data, and techniques used can vary greatly. Potential data sources can be a product that is chosen and its characteristics, users personal characteristics such as demographic data, past transactions, etc. (Ricci, Rokach, & Shapira, 2011). Burke (2007) describes six RS approaches that are listed here: 1) content-based, 2) knowledge-based, 3) community-based, 4) collaborative filtering-based, 5) demographic-based and 6) hybrid systems

(Burke, 2007). Out of these six approaches, knowledge-based recommendations and its sub-category constrained based recommender systems are described below as they form the theoretical basis for the design of the artifact.

2.4.1 Knowledge-Based and Constraint-Based Recommender Systems

Knowledge-based recommender systems (KRS) have specific domain knowledge on how certain item characteristics fit users' preferences. They do not require a significant amount of statistical data or information about the user and operate within the predefined knowledge base. KRS are ideal for scenarios where other relevant recommendation data sources are unavailable. They were particularly suitable for complex products where non-expert users do not have knowledge on item characteristics (Ricci et al., 2011). Furthermore, they are a commentary to other forms of RS, making them extendable to form future hybrid systems (Burke, 2007).

KRS can be implemented using two basic techniques that differ in the selection process used for the recommendations. The first technique uses case-based RS, where the KRS uses a similarity measure to compare items and their characteristics with user preferences. The second technique uses Constraint-based Recommender Systems (CRS). They convert user preferences into constraints based on rules formulated into the system. These constraints are used to filter out and select recommendations that are shown to users (Felfernig & Burke, 2008).

While research on KRS is to a much lesser extent in comparison to other RS variants, they still are highly relevant. CRS is a relatively popular form of KRS (Jannach, Zanker, Ge, & Gröning, 2012). As these RS rely heavily on the knowledge base and rules within the systems, the structure of the database and methods for entering data need to be planned and executed carefully.

Extracting user preferences from their interaction with the system is a challenge. Personalized interfaces that have optimized user interaction dialogs are one way of extracting user preferences. Another approach is using the critiquing technique, where users do not need to specify all of their requirements at the beginning of the process. Instead, they build their preferences by going through many recommendation cycles and giving their feedback at each step. In each iterative step, the system presents a small number of options and users can give their feedback. The user continues reviewing different iterations until a matching item is retrieved (Ricci et al., 2011).

This critiquing technique is similar, as there are also iterations with the use of a toolkit and its associated design questions. The design of the toolkit in this study follows the model of presenting recommendations based on a constraint-based knowledge base that is refined by iterative feedback. However, the toolkit should also be able to automate design steps and generate recommendable solutions. The upcoming chapters describe these techniques.

3 Method and Context

This chapter presents the method and data used to study how a toolkit that generates recommendations can simplify solution space and enable non-expert users. The chapter consists of three sections. The first section places the research approach followed in *Part IV* in the overall research approach of the thesis. The second section describes the research design by explaining in detail, the research method used and the various steps followed to design and evaluate the toolkit. The next chapters describe the artifacts and explain the results of the evaluation steps.

3.1 Research Approach

The research approach in *Part IV* builds upon the findings from *Part II* and *Part III* and addresses the overall research question from the perspective of designing a new solution. *Part II* looked at the human side of the research question by taking the users' perspective and studying user innovators and their innovations. *Part III* was also an exploratory study, but it narrowed down the scope of solution space from a user's solution space to the toolkit's solution space and studied the software (toolkit artifact) itself. *Part IV* aims at studying the interactions between the domains of the environment of toolkit use (outside) and the structure of the toolkit (inside). Figure 24 presents the research approach of *Part IV* in the overall context of the research approach of the thesis.

The real world context chosen for the study was toolkits to design storage cabinets. This choice has two reasons. Firstly, storage cabinets consist of modules of customizable shelves that are easy to visualize and adapt. Even in this seemingly simple context, the solution space is large enough to be simplified, as there are infinite permutations and combinations possible. Secondly, potential users can easily evaluate toolkit design in this context through experiments that compare usage of the new toolkit with traditional customizing toolkits. The following section explains the research design followed in *Part IV*.

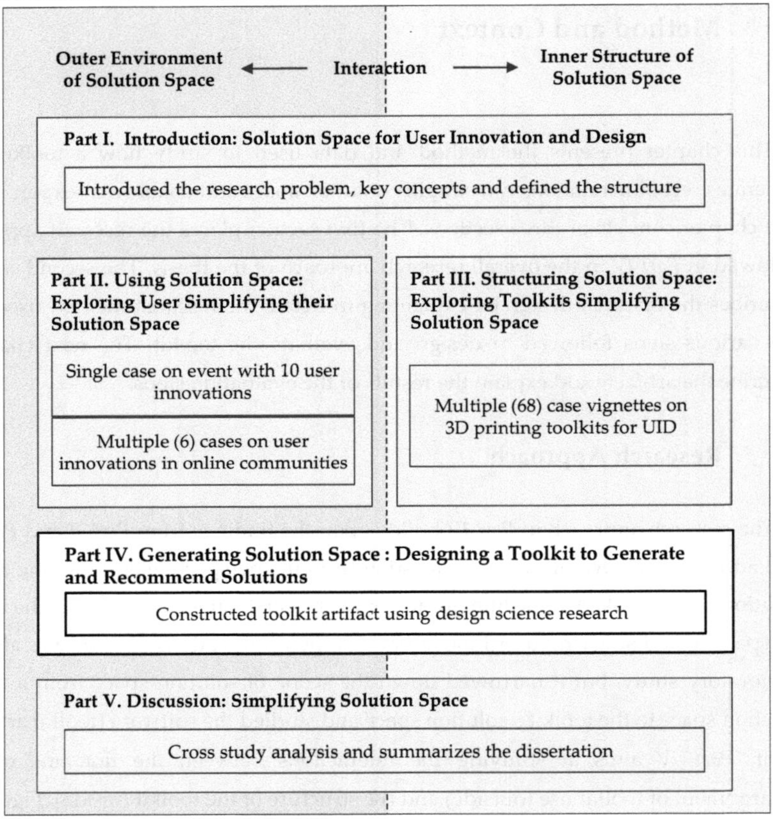

Figure 24: Part IV within the overall thesis research approach

3.2 Research Design

The research question of whether a toolkit that generates recommendations can simplify solution space and enable non-expert users is addressed by designing artifacts following design science research method. Design science research is a process to continuously build-and-evaluate and produces a set of artifacts (Hevner et al. 2004). The main goal was to develop artifacts that support toolkits that recommended solutions to users. Since recommending solutions to users based on their feedback is a novel approach, its design required iterative evaluation and refinement of the artifacts developed through the search process. Figure 25 describes the research design. It follows Peffers et al. (2007) and consists of six steps.

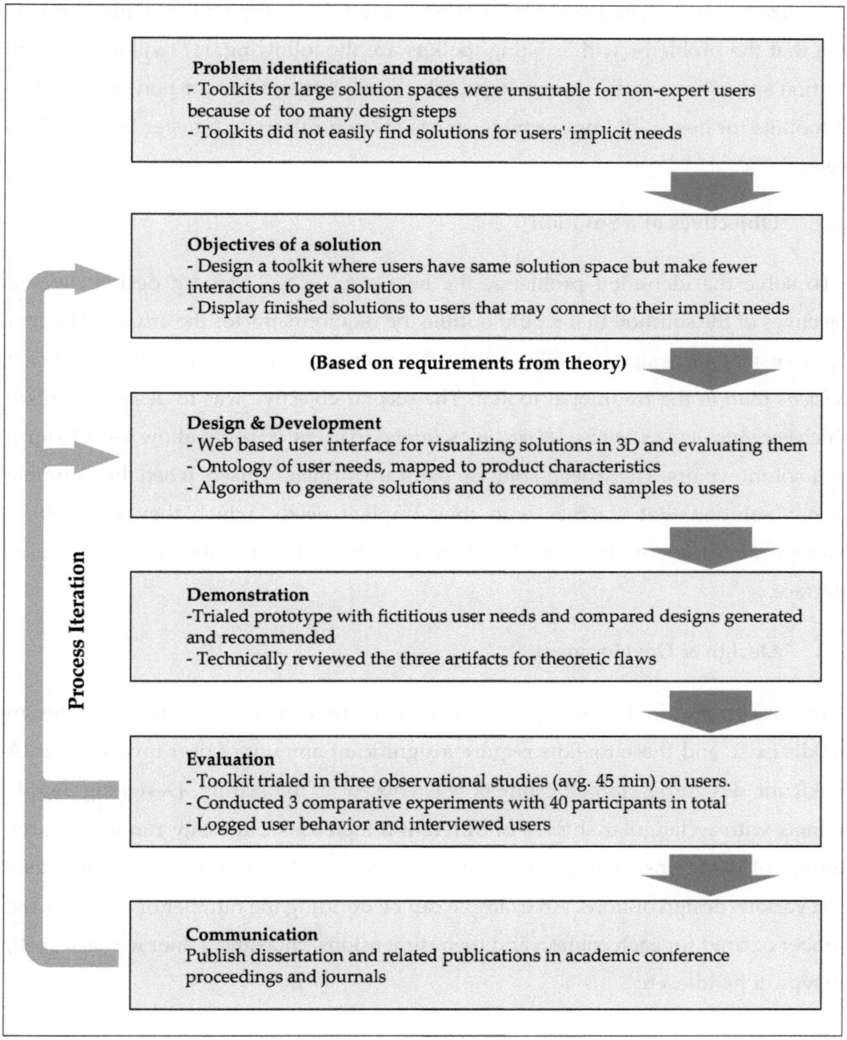

Figure 25: Research design based on DSR (Peffers & Tuunanen, 2007)

3.2.1 Problem Identification and Motivation

The first step of the research design was to identify the problem to be researched. After the two studies of *Part II* and *Part III*, a literature review on toolkits for mass customization and related concepts was conducted. From these three sources, it was seen that the problems with existing toolkits are the following: (1) toolkits for large solution space have many design steps, which was not suitable for non-expert users (2) toolkits for design did not provide an easy way for users to transfer their implicit needs.

3.2.2 Objectives of a Solution

To solve the identified problems, the next step of the research design defined objectives of the solution that would outline the requirements for the artifact. The first objective was to design a toolkit where the user will have to *perform fewer design decisions* than in the traditional toolkit. The second objective was to design a toolkit, which *generated and recommended possible solutions* to users. It would allow users to form need-solution pairs. These need-solution pairs are formed by users when they stumble upon a solution that matches with their implicit needs, which they were either unaware of earlier or they could not express through a traditional toolkit's user interface.

3.2.3 Design & Development

The design required choosing a context for the new toolkit, in which user design toolkits exist, and these toolkits require a significant amount of user involvement. A toolkit for designing storage cabinets was chosen as the setting. Designing simple cabinets with rectangular shelves of different dimensions can easily run into a large number of variations. In a traditional toolkit, users make multiple design decisions with various design options. An example can be deciding the number of columns, the number of rows for each column and their dimensions, choosing a door for each shelf, the type of handle, etc.

Building a generative design toolkit is a new concept, but draws upon various fields, the artifact requirements were inferred from theoretical foundations in the areas of user design toolkits and mass-customization systems. This knowledge and techniques stem from the area of recommender systems, and they are adapted for the purpose of design toolkits.

Based on these theoretical foundations, a prototype web-based toolkit for users to select predesigned storage cabinets was developed. The cabinets were designed by the toolkit to match users' explicit and implicit needs. The prototype web-based toolkit consists of three artifacts: 1) a web-based front end user interface for presenting recommended solutions and visualizing them in 3D 2) an ontology of user need functions mapped to product characteristics, and 3) an algorithm to traverse through the solution space, generate solutions, and recommend appropriate samples to users.

3.2.4 Demonstration

For the purpose of demonstration, the toolkit was trialed using fictitious user needs, and the resulting designs were checked with the configured specifications to identify and eliminate any technical errors. The generated solutions and recommendations were also logged at major steps of the algorithm and compared to ensure that the artifacts functioned as per their theoretical design. The user interface was also tested with various boundary conditions to see if they were correctly displayed. These steps formed the technical review of the artifacts that ensured they operated as intended at a theoretical level.

3.2.5 Evaluation

Evaluation of the artifacts was conducted using two forms. Preliminary evaluation of the artifacts was performed using observational studies on users, at regular intervals. The trials involved three observational studies, each with one user and two observers. In each of the six studies, the user was observed while using the toolkit, for approximately 20 minutes and their usage behavior was logged. The user was then also interviewed with various open-ended questions that explored the user's usage perceptions at different stages of the trial with the toolkit. Each user was also asked for feedback on the construction of the toolkit, which guided the design of the artifacts. Iterative cycles of demonstration to potential users of the toolkit contributed to fine tuning the toolkit and building its design knowledge.

Further to the demonstrations to individual users and observing their usage, the toolkit was also evaluated by performing experiments on users. These experiments had a single-case research design (Christensen, 2007), where the same set of participants used the designed prototype toolkit as well as a traditional customization toolkit where users could design a storage cabinet by themselves. Three experiments were conducted in all with a sum of 40 participants, and descriptive techniques of data analysis were conducted. The experiments were followed by a workshop where the participants discussed their usage of both the toolkits and suggested features to improve them. It provided further qualitative data, which was used to improve the toolkit further and improve the comparison between the toolkits. The results of the evaluations are also presented in this study.

3.2.6 Communication

The design science research method (Peffers & Tuunanen, 2007) stresses on communicating the knowledge resulting from the study. This study has research contributions in the field of toolkits for user innovation and design. Hence, publishing the study in relevant conference proceedings and journals is a future step after publishing this dissertation to highlight the problem, its importance, the novelty, and utility of the artifact, the rigor of its design and its effectiveness.

4 Findings: Describing the Artifacts

This chapter presents the first part of the results of the study conducted using design science research, the artifacts that resulted in the design process. The DSR study constructed three artifacts that together form the ***Feedback based IteRative Solutions Toolkit*** (**FIRST**)[21] a web application toolkit, to meet the objectives of this study. FIRST is a toolkit to customize storage cabinets for the non-expert user. It is based on an algorithm that generated all solutions in the solution set and then using a critique based recommender system to recommend solution samples to users. The advantage of this toolkit is that it designs the solutions for the user and focusses navigation for the user by only presenting solutions that are likely to match user preferences. Non-expert users also interact with finished solutions rather than design their solutions from scratch. Therefore, they are inclined to select a solution that is good enough rather than stop the design process before findings a satisfactory solution.

Designing the toolkit needed a well-defined architecture that allowed it to be functional while being flexible to improvements and maintenance activities. The model-view-controller architecture pattern was adopted which separated the toolkit into three layers: the model layer, the view layer, and the controller layer (Leff & Rayfield, 2001). Model-view-controller (MVC)[22] is a programming model and implementation infrastructure that allows the design of the toolkit in a flexible manner. It allows modifications to the partitioning of the toolkit, which is usually made in the initial stages of design. Its key idea is to separate the user interface, the underlying data behind the user interface and the logic controlling the application. Following this approached allowed drastically changing the application's look and feel without changing the data structures and business logic as much. Each of the three artifacts of the study corresponds to a layer of the toolkit. The separation of the layers and their

---

[21] The development version of FIRST is demonstrated at http://reconfig.class.wi1projects.com

[22] The MVC design pattern is also known as the Presentation-Abstraction-Control (PAC) design pattern (Coutaz, 1987)

interconnections are shown in Figure 26. The following sections further describe the three artifacts.

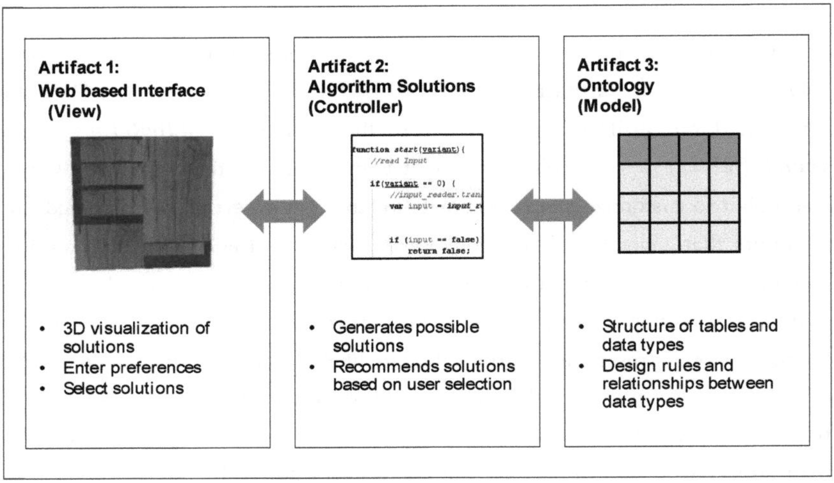

Figure 26: Three artifacts following the MVC pattern (Leff & Rayfield, 2001)

4.1 Artifact 1: Web-based Interface (View)

This section describes the first artifact, which is the prototype user interface of FIRST, the feedback based toolkit that this study constructed. The traditional model of the toolkit as conceptualized by Hippel and Katz (2002) provides users the ability to learn by doing through trial and error cycles. FIRST, on the other hand, learns about the user's needs through trial and error cycles of suggesting different designs to the user. FIRST explicitly asked some of the user needs are through a basic form while it inferred the other implicit needs from the user's choices. This method leads to the incremental building of the user's needs through the selection process followed in the toolkit.

This selection process follows the critiquing method to interact with users. This method is adopted from knowledge-based recommender systems (KRS), a type of constraint-based recommender systems (CRS) mentioned earlier. This method, initially found in case-based reasoning for conversational dialogs is also used in KRS and CRS (Burke, 2007) While they are used to present users with different options of products so that they can provide feedback by critiquing the options, FIRST presents users a sample of generated solutions and collects feedback on them. It used this feedback to identify implicit needs and match them to design characteristics of the solution.

As the point of contact of the underlying layers with the user, it has an especially important role in the design of the toolkit FIRST. In such a scenario, it is important to use lightweight and modern technologies, i.e., they give users a quick response time in their interactions. The web interface is browser-based. It generates and filters solutions as well as visualizes them in 3D. It is explained below systematically along with a simplified flow chart.

1. The toolkit assumes that users have explicit and implicit needs, which it needs to capture to find users matching solutions. On accessing the toolkit URL, FIRST asks users for their explicit needs, which they can enter by filling up a form. They can enter height, width, and depth of their needed cabinet and choose between one more functional needs they expect to fulfill with the cabinet.

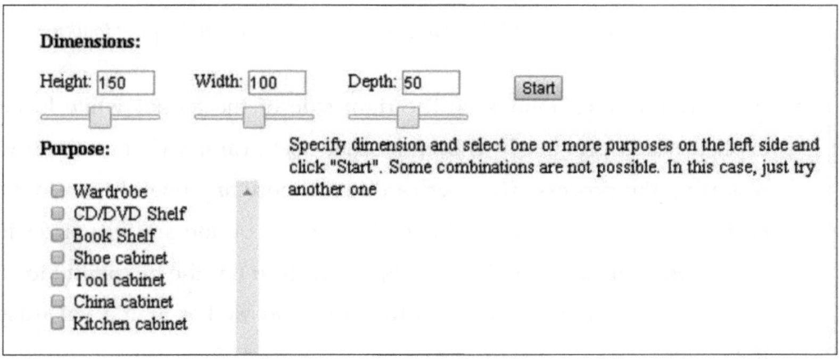

Figure 27: Input form for explicit needs

On clicking start, FIRST converts the chosen explicit needs into design criteria that act as constraints for the solution and then generates a large sample of representative solutions from the constraint bounded solution set. It then makes a pre-selection of nine solutions (optimal number of options from user evaluations) from this large sample set and presents them to the user.

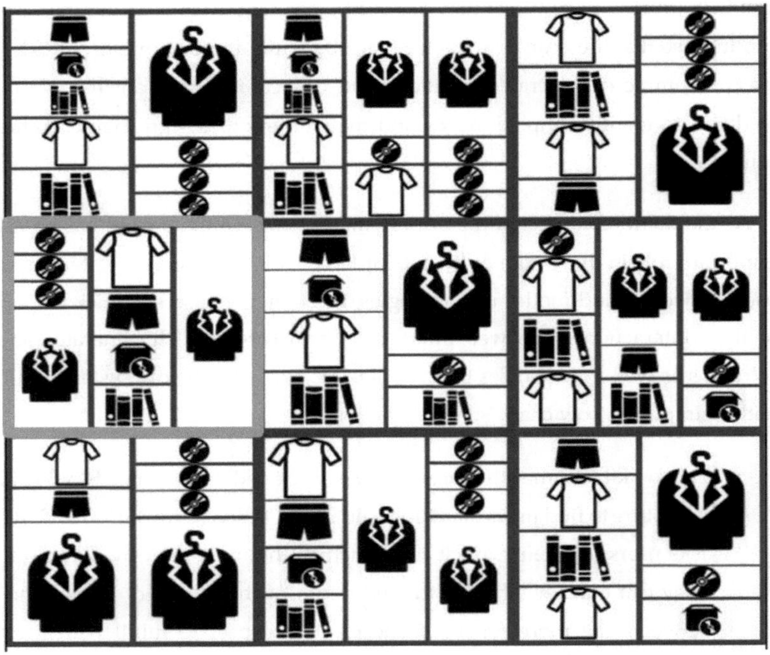

Figure 28: Nine sampled solutions generated by the toolkit

2. It shows the nine options on the right side of the toolkit while locking the explicit needs previously chosen so that users cannot change them without restarting the process. The user can then choose any one of these options by clicking on them. FIRST highlights the selected option and visualizes it in 3D on the left using a 3D rendering engine. The user has the possibility to zoom in and pan the 3D representation of the cabinet as well as toggle a 2D display of the cabinet.

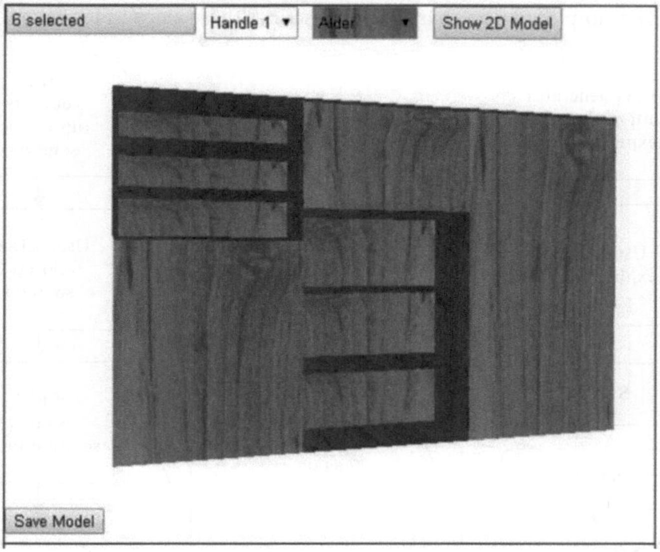

Figure 29: Visualization of selection option in the browser in 3D

3. The user can then re-click on the option to generate solutions similar to the one selected. On performing this step, FIRST stores the characteristics of the selected model as implicit needs and uses them to calculate new solution recommendations for the user. FIRST displays the implicit needs that are stored on top of the options, so that users can always erase any of the implicit needs that were wrongly stored by the toolkit.
4. In addition to the feedback-based interface, FIRST also allows users to change certain product characteristics that are expected to remain the same irrespective of the generated recommendations. These characteristics are the type of material used for the cabinet and the handles that are used. Changing them does not affect the generated solutions and associated recommendations.
5. Users can at any point of time save multiple designs that they like and view them later. Hence, the user can potentially run through many sets of iterations and save all designs that they find interesting before revisiting them and deciding which design(s) they would finally like to purchase.

The simplified flowchart below describes these steps in Figure 30.

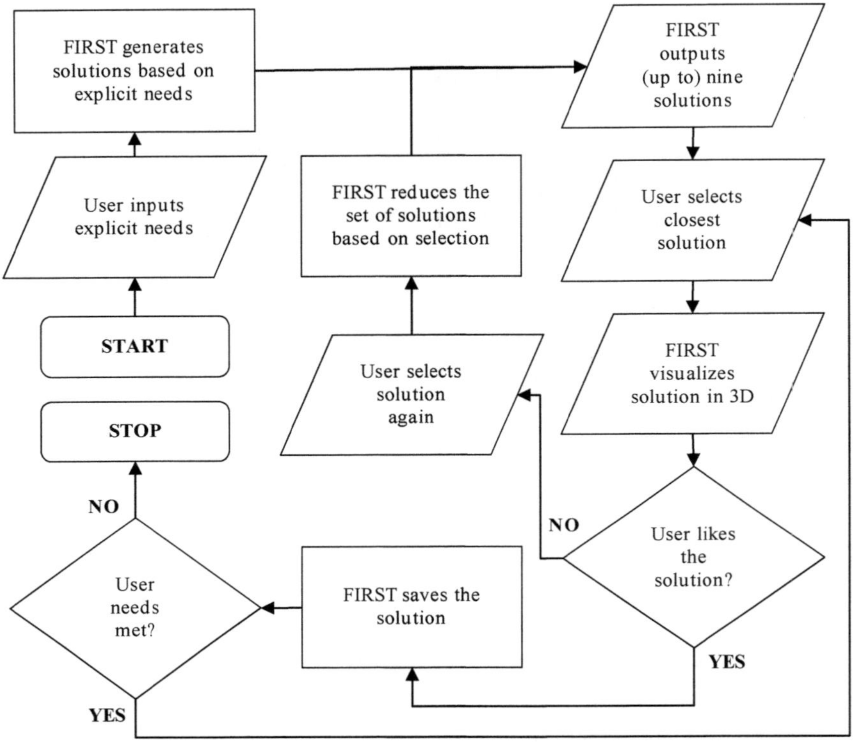

Figure 30: Simplified flowchart of user interactions with FIRST

4.2 Artifact 2: Algorithm for Solutions (Controller)

FIRST relies on an algorithm with three parts for generating different solutions and filtering them based on user feedback. The first part validates the explicit needs directly entered by the user. The second part generates solutions based on the explicit needs. The third part deals with the reduction of the solutions into the sample presented to the user and filters out gradually solutions based on implicit needs of the users. The second and third parts of the algorithm are directly related to constraint-based recommender systems (CRS) discussed earlier in Chapter 2. CRS creates the appropriate knowledge base and matches the appropriate solutions to provide as recommendations. The knowledge base is a set of variables and a set of constraints. The variables consist of attributes of the user and the design, while the constraints can be in the form of filters on explicit instantiations of solutions (Felfernig, Friedrich, & Schmidt-Thieme, 2007). Constraint-based matching typically uses backtracking to find suitable solutions, which this algorithm also uses. With this approach, it follows a depth-first-search principle and defines variables and checks for validity at each step. Solutions which emerge are stored, but in other cases, when it hits the depth (i.e., reaches an invalid combination) it takes a step back and tries a different value for the previously selected variable. These three parts are explained in further detail below.

4.2.1 Explicit needs Validation

As a user first uses the toolkit and enters in the explicit needs, the algorithm validates the entered explicit needs. Stored rules that define maximum sets of valid combinations validate the explicit needs. These maximum sets are stored in the explicit database, and they show combinations of elements that are valid.

4.2.2 Solution Generation

Each solution is a cabinet that consists of components of elemental shapes, which are building blocks of the cabinets. The building blocks map to different functionalities entered in the explicit needs, and their dimensions are modifiable within certain tolerance levels. The algorithm generates all possible sequences of combinations of these blocks that match the criteria given to them. For example, one wardrobe shelf and two shoe shelves is a generated sequence as it could fit into a cabinet of dimensions 100cmX100cmX50cm.

The dimensions of the cabinet determined the number of columns in the cabinet. This step is a constraint enforced upon the toolkit for aesthetic reasons and it, in turn, streamlines the task of fitting in the building blocks into the cabinet. Once the columns are set, the next task is to insert the modules into the defined columns of the cabinet.

This step is a simple 'box matching' algorithm that follows a recursive trial and error principle similar to a depth-first search. It attempts to find a solution by inserting the modules into the predefined columns and saves every successful attempt as a solution model. If not, then it modifies the modules within their tries again.

Once the algorithm assembles the modules, the cabinet can have further variations in the form of individual customizations of open or closed doors, types of inner drawers, etc. These variations are recursively generated after the other implicit needs have already restricted the designs considerably. As these needs are finer variations, FIRST presents these variations to the user only as the last step in the process.

4.2.3 Solution Reduction

Once the solution generating algorithm has generated different solutions, the next part of the algorithm samples the solutions and selects those that are the most appropriate to the user. To be able to achieve this, the algorithm attempts to show users a limited set of solutions with the greatest diversity. The algorithm creates a set of buckets to categorize different solutions based on characteristics that identified to create the most diversity. It then distributes all solutions across these buckets. Once it has distributed the solutions, it picks one solution from each bucket by calculating the solution that has the farthest distance from the average of the solutions of the bucket.

The algorithm calculates the distance by comparing different sequences that are part of each solution. For example, if a sequence was x1, x2, ... x9, and the average was represented by the sequence m1, m2, ... m9. Then the distance from the average is:

$$Distance = (x1-m1)^2 + (x2-m2)^2 + \ldots. +(x9-m9)^2$$

Along with this calculation, once an entry is stored in the implicit database that represents the user's implicit need, the algorithm uses the entry to filter out all solutions that do not meet this implicit need.

4.3 Artifact 3: Ontology for Need-based Recommendations (Model)

Constructing FIRST requires a *conceptualization* of user needs and design characteristics of storage cabinets (Genesereth & Nilsson, 1987). The conceptualization draws from objects, concepts, entities, and their relationships in the area of user needs and design, derived from literature and theory discussed in Chapter 2. This conceptualization forms the abstract, simplified view that is used to represent the world. The conceptualization is explicitly specified in information systems using an ontology. An ontology is a formal specification of the types, properties, and interrelationships of the entities that represents the relevant topics in existence[23]. By defining an ontology to represent, there is a common vocabulary that represents the conceptualization which can guarantee consistency between different agents applying this knowledge (Gruber, 1995). Hence, an ontology for need-based recommendations is an artifact that can be used in future applications of information systems.

The needs-based recommendations ontology is a representation of needs and solutions and other concepts that are a part of the toolkit. It stores needs and rules connecting them to design characteristics in FIRST, the toolkit that was developed. While FIRST is a toolkit for customizing cabinets, the ontology has components that can be generalized to other scenarios where users give feedback by visual interaction with the solutions recommended by the toolkit. The ontology consists of classes that divided into three groups, namely data classes, presentation classes and logic classes.

Three main data classes relate to the data stored in the toolkit used for solutions generation and recommendations. These are the explicit database, implicit database, and model classes. These classes represent the constraints used to filter out only those cabinets that meet user needs and represent the cabinets themselves. Two additional classes: history and log manager are used for additional functionalities of the toolkit such as saving finished designs and logging user interactions.

The view classes consist of input reader, output writer, and object visualizer. The classes deal with input forms where the user can enter explicit needs, representation of generated options and visualization of a selected solution in 3D. The object visualizer class also uses open source JavaScript 3D rendering libraries WebGL and Three.js.

---

[23] The term ontology originates from philosophy, where an Ontology is a systematic account of being, existence, or reality. It includes structures of objects, properties, events, processes and relations in reality (Smith, 2003).

The logic classes include model calculator and model reducer, which mainly consist of functions that generate different solutions and reduce them into the set of up to nine solutions shown to the user in each iteration.

While all the classes listed above are critical to the functioning of the toolkit, a few of them are highlighted because they deal directly with the needs and recommendations. Key classes of the above three groups are described in further detail.

4.3.1 Explicit Database

The explicit database is the class used to store all the information about explicit user needs that users can themselves enter into the toolkit. It also includes all the fixed parameters that have been set in the toolkit that users cannot normally modify. The calculations need these parameters, and the toolkit administrator can modify them as required. Explicit needs entered by users can be stored directly in the form of cabinet characteristics such as height, width, depth, material, handle, etc. It also includes parameters set by converting the explicit needs into design parameters using rules within the toolkit. These rules affect minimum and maximum conditions of the dimensions, constraints on the compatibility of different elements, etc. Table 14.presents detailed characteristics of the explicit database.

4.3.2 Implicit database

The implicit database is used to store all the need information that user does not explicitly enter but are identified by FIRST during the iterative selection process. FIRST builds the implicit needs using preference construction theory, to identify option preferences sub-consciously selected by the user. Qualitative feedback during evaluations ranked the elements in the implicit database class on their importance. Users listed design characteristics that differentiated between different solutions. These characteristics were recorded from user solutions with a higher priority. The structure of the implicit database is described in further detail in Table 15.

Table 14: Structure of Explicit Needs Database

Variables	Description
height, width, depth	Dimensions of the current model
Min-height, max-height, min-width, max-width, min-depth, max-depth	Minimum and maximum conditions of the dimensions
Handle-type, Material-type	Initial values for handles and material
Rows constraint	Physical constraints, specifying the number of rows that a model can contain, given a set of dimensions
Functional-constraints	Functional constraints, specifying different functional types of elements through values, such as standard height, maximum height tolerance, possible door options and hierarchical level
Selected-Functions	Function and purpose options that are selected by the user in the interface
Valid-Door-Combinations	Door constraints, specifying the possible door options for all elements globally
Combinations-Limit-Rules	Compatibility constraints, defining all possible combinations of purpose functions through maximum sets

Table 15: Structure of Implicit Needs Database

Variables	Description
Row number	Number of rows
Implicit-needs-order	Weighting of the model (ratio between different technical functions)
Elements-order	Build version, specified through the values and hierarchical version
Handle, material, door	Selected handle, material and door options

4.3.3 Input Reader

The input reader class contains all elements related to user modification of the generated solutions. It collects explicit needs from the user and visualizes the identified implicit needs for the user. This class also validates the explicit needs entered by the user by checking on the dimensions entered and the purpose functions selected. Therefore, this class can be considered an interface class, that is in between users and the other classes and strongly tied with model calculation.

Once FIRST validates the explicit needs, the input reader contains rules that translate user needs into design parameters and store them into the explicit database. So for example, an explicit need of a wardrobe would mean that FIRST chooses design parameter IDs 0.2.3 while an explicit need of a shoe storage will mean that FIRST chooses the parameter ID 1. These IDs are converted to valid option intervals for underlying design parameters and define the boundaries between which solutions can be generated by the algorithm.

4.3.4 Solution Model

Each cabinet solution that is generated is stored using the solution model. It contains all the necessary elements to that store the dimensions of the cabinet. The cabinet model is linked to other structures for options that are specific to the different parts of the cabinet (such as doors). They have variables indicating the elemental blocks, their dimensions, as well as handle and material details.

5 Findings: Evaluations

Chapter 5 presents the second part of the results of this study. *Part IV* follows design science research method, with the aim of solving the research problem of simplifying solution space for non-expert users by designing artifacts. The evaluation of these artifacts forms a critical activity of the research method as it provides critical feedback to the design process and indicates how well the artifact supports the problem. FIRST was evaluated on a regular basis during the design process, as well as after the prototype reached a stable version to evaluate certain hypothesis proposed for the study. The study conducted two types of evaluation activities. The first were a set of three preliminary observational studies done on users of the toolkit, during the design process. It was followed by three experiments conducted on participants who used a traditional toolkit for creating custom cabinets and compared it with FIRST. These evaluation activities carried out on the artifacts are presented in the following sections.

5.1 Observational Studies

One of the first evaluations done was an observational study with a potential user in a workshop that lasted 60 minutes. This study showed that the user found too many options at each step confusing and it had to be limited. Furthermore, the importance of showing significant variations between the options became apparent. Users implicit needs needed to be set in an order based on the importance to users so that they can quickly filter them out through their selections and focus on the minor variations. The user also pointed out suggestions to improve the model visualization and validated add-on features such as a save function to store the currently selected model and to scale up the 3D design whenever required. This feedback was implemented through many updates to the toolkit.

The second user evaluation was another 30-minute workshop. This workshop also validated some of the feedback received from the previous evaluation regarding better visualization of the 3D model and better diversity in the recommendations. The user also provided further inputs on the type of explicit needs, their corresponding purposes, and design features and gave further ideas on better presentation of the solutions.

A third user evaluation study was conducted with two users, where each used the toolkit for around 20 minutes. One of the users had a clear idea of the design of the cabinet required while the other did not have a clear goal in mind. Both were optimistic of the toolkit model where finished solutions are recommended to users. The user with clear needs required more interaction possibilities and wanted the toolkit to be less restrictive, while the other user liked the diversity in different solutions. They both also preferred some of the additional features created such as the toggle between 2D and 3D and saving solutions into a history.

5.2 Experiments

This section is a summative report on three experiments conducted as part of the evaluation of the prototype toolkit, FIRST. The three experiments involved participants using FIRST and a traditional customizing toolkit to design storage cabinets based on their needs. The experiments suggest that participants with fewer explicit needs quickly arrive at solutions with FIRST that satisfy their needs while those with clearly defined explicit needs were not satisfied by the solutions generated by FIRST. In the following sections, the experimental method is first explained in further detail. It is then followed by a presentation of the results.

5.2.1 Method

5.2.1.1 Participants

To evaluate the performance of FIRST in simplifying solution space for non-expert users, 41 participants were selected from the local university campus in Germany. The participants were between ages 23 and 30 and included nine female participants. The participants were all from a non-engineering background, but at the same time technically literate and interested in information technology. They were all familiar with the concepts of mass customization prior to the experiments, through either their education or their experiences. However, they all had no prior experience in designing storage cabinets with toolkits. Hence, these participants were selected as non-experts for the study. They were also involved in the purchase of cabinets in the past and so could identify specific needs when selecting or designing a solution.

5.2.1.2 Apparatus

The experiments had the participants use two web-based toolkits. One of which is FIRST that was already described. The second toolkit was a traditional customizer (TC)[24] for designing storage cabinets that followed a traditional user interface. TC has a user interface where the user makes sequential design decisions and selects options at each step. The user first enters the overall dimensions of the cabinet and then decides the number of columns for the cabinet and the number of rows for each column. A snapshot of TC can be seen in Figure 31.Both the toolkits had every user action logged. After completing the process of designing or selecting a solution, the toolkit page redirected to an on-line survey.

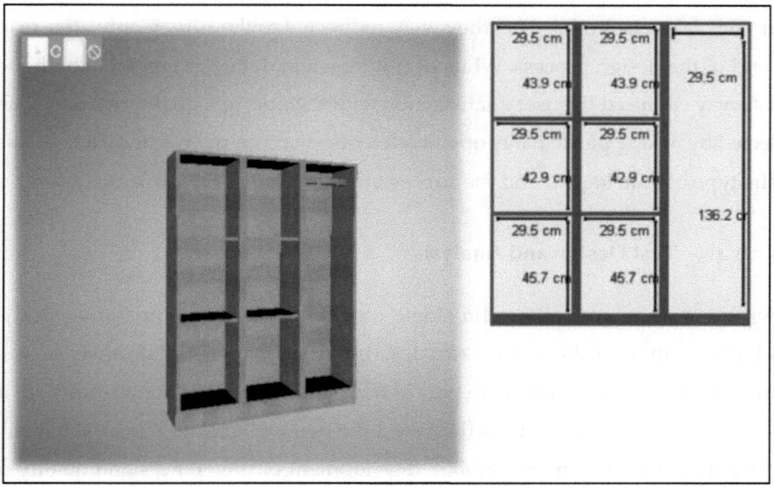

Figure 31: Screenshot of the traditional customizer toolkit (TC)

[24] The development version of TC is demonstrated at http://oldconfig.class.wi1projects.com

5.2.1.3 Procedure

The three experiments followed a single-case experimental design. Therefore, the same group of participants first used the traditional configurator and then after they had finished, used the new toolkit. In both cases, the users were given detailed instructions before they started to use the toolkits. The participants were asked to put themselves in the position of a customer looking to buy storage cabinets based on their specific needs. They were encouraged to explore the toolkits and ask questions for clarification. The participants were also briefly introduced to the concept of toolkits for user innovation and design and given a quick introduction to the toolkits' main functionalities.

Participants were initially asked to design their customized storage cabinets with FIRST. It allowed them to save multiple designs and users were free to complete the process whenever they were ready or to keep designing. On completing the design process, they filled in an online survey. The participants then used TC and designed their own cabinets. In this case, they were redirected to the survey only after reaching the end of the design process. While user interaction data was logged in both toolkits and survey captured the user's satisfaction with their design, qualitative data was also collected by asking participants open-ended questions on the two toolkits. The details on the type of data logged and the survey questions are in the Appendix.

5.2.1.4 Test Design and Analysis

As the experiments followed a single case design and a comparative study was conducted with two different toolkits, descriptive techniques of data analysis were the primary goals for the quantitative part of the evaluation. Evaluation results are in the form of path analysis of users as they used the two toolkits and the survey results on user's perception of using the toolkit, development of preferences and quality of the solutions found at the end. Qualitative answers were also collected from the feedback workshops conducted as the final stage of the experiments.

The quantitative variables of importance in the evaluation were the following:

1) Time taken to reach a solution: This variable was calculated from the user logs as they used each toolkit.

2) User confidence in the solution: This variable was calculated from users' response (using a 5-point Likert scale) to three statements in the survey[25].

These variables led to the following hypothesis:

H1: Users can find solutions faster with toolkits that generate and recommend solutions than traditional toolkits.

H2: Users can find better solutions with toolkits that generate and recommend solutions provided than traditional toolkits.

5.2.2 Results

5.2.2.1 Path Analysis

The figures show typical path models users take when working with the two toolkits. The horizontal axis represents time passed from when the user started the design process. The vertical axis has the different levels of the customization process. In line with the very different approaches to solution space in the two toolkits, users follow completely different paths when using them. This section makes a few brief comments by comparing the occurrence of trial-and-error cycles and time periods involved. A more detailed comparison between the two toolkits can be found in the Annex.

When using the Traditional Customizer (TC), users have a clear direction they follow with sequential design decisions. There are very few trial-and-error cycles, which only occur at the end of the design process. Some of the users did not complete the design and just stopped the process. It is in contrast with FIRST, where users are already working with completed designs and through their selections, the toolkit

25 The three items in the survey were "I was able to design my own cabinet", "I need more variety to design my own cabinet" and "The final cabinet fits with my personal impression of a cabinet"

quickly identifies their implicit preferences and goes through a few cycles of unselecting and selecting the implicit needs it determines.

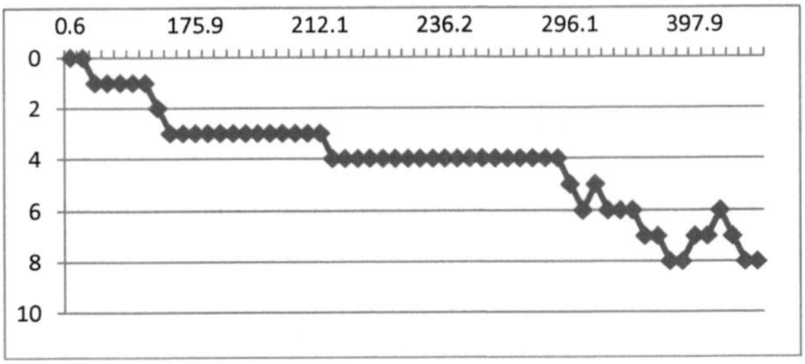

Figure 32: Typical user path when using the Traditional Customizer

The time taken to find a solution using FIRST were considerably lower than using

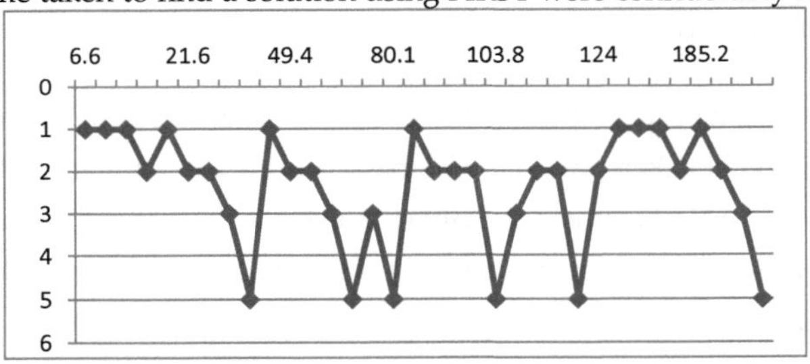

Figure 33: Standard user path model when using FIRST

TC, but there was a significant variation. Users of TC needed much time to complete the first few steps and then on began to shorten the time with each step. It implied that the TC needed some time before users could comprehend the configuration process and start working. The structure of the TC also forced users to perform many more design decisions. On the other hand, in the case of FIRST, users could finish the first step of entering their explicit needs relatively quickly and spent more time trying to improve their models. Some users quickly finished the design process while the others spent longer in exploring different solutions to pick one that exactly fit their needs. Users in both toolkits spent considerable time on selecting the different material and door options, implying a strong desire to influence directly the model through their interactions.

Analyzing user behavior through their logged interactions with the toolkit provides valuable insights on user behavior. Although the size of the experiments and a large number of unaccounted variables limit the generalizability of the findings, they encourage future quantitative studies in this regard. T-test results on the show that two-tailed P value equals 0.0029, showing that the difference was extremely statistically significant. These results indicate that the first hypothesis *H1 (Users can find solutions faster with toolkits that generate and recommend solutions than traditional toolkits)* is supported.

Table 16: Time taken for users to find/design their solutions

	FIRST	*TC*
Mean	178.505	358.0544
Std. Dev	167.5154	192.3106
Count	38	35

5.2.2.2 Survey

The users were redirected to a survey after they finished using each of the two toolkits. The redirection happened after they completed the design process in the case of the TC, while they were free to stop using the toolkit and enter the survey any time they liked with FIRST. The survey consisted of nine Likert-type items, which can be seen in the Annex D. There were twenty and twenty-one responses for the TC and FIRST respectively.

On calculating the means of the survey responses, the data did not give conclusive responses for all question but provided valuable leads that can be followed with future research. Users who were able to complete the design process with the TC firmly believed they had designed their cabinet (75%), while with FIRST they were not so sure (23%). The 50% of the users of FIRST changed their responses during the design process while only 30% of TC users did so. Hence, the second hypothesis *H2 (Users can find better solutions with toolkits that generate and recommend solutions provided than traditional toolkits)* was not supported.

5.2.2.3 Workshop Discussion

A 15-minute workshop session was conducted with the participants in each of the experiments to understand their logged activity and survey responses better and get qualitative inputs through statements on their experiences and feedback. It gave a better understanding of the participants' decision-making process and feelings when using the toolkits. The feedback from the users who were very involved with their design supported the survey results that the recommended solutions from FIRST did not always fit their needs. However, in general, they were more favorable to the TC because it was at a much more advanced stage regarding usability to FIRST. They also felt that the personal bond of creating the model, which comes by being involved in the systematic design, was missing. However, they found the recommended solutions to be excellent starting points from which they could optimize their designs.

Nevertheless, users who did not have strong preferences for the cabinets were happy to spend a lesser time to get to a solution and were satisfied by the generated solutions. Some participants also did not fill up the survey for the TC because they could not complete the design process. These participants were, on the other hand, able to select a solution that was good enough for them using FIRST.

6 Discussion

This chapter presents a summary of all the results of the DSR study and ties it back to the research question. A new type of toolkit was designed (based on three artifacts) that is a novel exaptation of critique based constraint recommender systems for the use of toolkits for user innovation and design. This design was evaluated by conducting three experiments with potential users and conducting qualitative workshops. This chapter presents the summarized form of the design artifacts and general findings of the study and connects them to existing research.

6.1 General Discussions

This section reflects on the design process, technical aspects and elaborates more on the learnings. The designed toolkit FIRST is positioned as an 'exaptation,' by taking the tried and tested known solution of recommender systems into the new problem area of toolkits for user innovation and design (Gregor & Hevner, 2013). The DSR method involved performing many iterative development cycles, which were constantly evaluated. Including many evaluation points into the design cycles were invaluable in identifying user needs and ensuring that the designed artifact continued to be aimed at solving the identified problem. Feedback from these evaluation studies also brought challenges in design as the user interface and architecture had to be frequently changed.

6.1.1 Reflections

As the identified problem and research question heavily influenced the design, the toolkit had a flexible architecture. The toolkit ran on web browsers and using web-based JavaScript libraries with much processing done on the client side. This flexibility came at the cost of following formal architectures, optimized towards performance. Scaling up this toolkit to scenarios with a lot more generated solutions may require performance optimizations to handle different variations.

The evaluation results show that toolkits based on recommendations were considered in general as a novel approach and helpful to the non-expert user. In terms of focused navigation, FIRST was a better approach than the TC. It had inconclusive results in terms of user satisfaction. The generated solutions seem to be an excellent way to generate solutions as starting points when the user has very predefined needs or for complicated design decisions that non-expert user would rather not take part. The users who had a need in mind also wanted the ability to modify the generated solutions directly, even if it was by using simple functions such as scaling the cabinet. Not providing this capability risked negative reaction towards the toolkit that outweighed the benefits.

It implies that most of the users have a strong desire to influence the model directly through their interactions. One potential reason for this could be the personal experience of the users, who are more familiar with making direct choices than relying on recommendations. Another reason could be the higher relative importance of these options compared to the others – an opinion that surfaced later in the free discussion round where the test candidates liked the recommendations in the initial stage, but soon felt restricted by the limited interaction possibilities. The survey showed that a majority of the users changed their preferences during the configuration process. It is in line with the literature on preference construction during the customization process.

The toolkit has clear managerial implications in today's context of flexible production technologies such as various additive manufacturing technologies and modular embedded electronics. This large solution space is not readily available to users who are not willing to become experts. The artifacts developed in this study can be migrated to other contexts to generate new combinations of solutions to assist non-expert users. A toolkit that generates solutions can let users focus either partially or entirely on their preferences of complete solutions rather than always design from scratch.

6.1.2 Limitations and Future Research

The study has various limitations, some of which can be reduced following further iterations of the study. The design of the ontologies can be made more generalizable into contexts that are more complex and evaluated. Creating an ontology system that can be used in multiple context areas would be an ideal result. The experiments conducted to evaluate the toolkit follow a single case study design have a tendency of showing carry-over and order effects, where the results from one experiment phase carry-over into the next step and affect its results. Further experiments could follow different designs to avoid these. The user interface of FIRST needs to be also improved to provide effective guidance, which is essential for the success of toolkits in the case of non-experts. The experiments conducted as part of the evaluation studies were relatively small and homogenous, and this affects the generalizability of the results gained. Future research can continuously conduct experiments with a larger number of participants for better generalizability of the results. Another approach could be to distribute the toolkit among online communities of potential users and get a larger sample size of participants for quantitative research on discovering implicit needs.

6.2 Summary of Results

6.2.1 Designed Artifacts

This study answered the research question of how toolkits with recommendations can simplify solution space and enable non-expert users by designing artifacts following the DSR method. Three artifacts were designed which when put together form a web-based toolkit for designing cabinets that satisfy user needs. The toolkit operates differently from similar toolkits used traditionally for customization by generating solutions and recommending them to users. Users can directly state their explicit needs or indirectly state their implicit needs by selecting the solutions closest to what they need. The toolkit identifies implicit needs based on their selections and uses it to refine the solutions and provide better recommendations to the user.

6.2.2 Hypotheses Validation

The experiments conducted as part of design evaluation were not extensive enough to validate the hypothesis. However, the results in the form of data logs, surveys, and workshop discussions give us various clues on how the hypothesis can be validated in the future. The summarized results are categorized under each of the four hypotheses.

Hypothesis 1 stated that toolkits that recommended solutions guide users faster to their required solutions. This hypothesis is supported, and the mean times with FIRST are considerably lower than the man times for finding a solution with the TC. Also, it was seen that the average number of interactions between the user and the toolkit needed with FIRST were considerably lower than the average number of interactions in the case of the TC. The qualitative responses suggest non-expert users with non-specific needs are happy with the quality of recommended solutions provided by FIRST. However, the opposite effect was seen with users with very specific needs, especially when the solutions provided were not diverse enough.

Hypothesis H2 stated that toolkits based on recommended solutions are perceived to be better than with a traditional toolkit. It was not supported in the data, and both toolkits received negative ratings regarding ease of use. The average score of FIRST was even lower than that of TC. However, the workshop discussions revealed that the confusion was not due to recommended solutions to the toolkit, but the lack of guidance and explanation on the toolkit for new users. They suggested more help-text, which appears in the form of tooltips or clearer instructions at the start as possible improvements to the toolkit.

6.3 Conclusion

Part IV of the thesis followed the DSR method to construct an artifact, a toolkit aimed to simplify solution space for non-expert users. It used learnings from *Part II* and *Part III,* and literature on problem formulation of implicit needs to construct a toolkit that generated and recommended solutions to non-expert users. Theory of recommender systems formed a basis for the design. The design was evaluated using observational studies and experiments with potential users. It was seen that designed toolkit brought more focused navigation to users thus simplifying their solution space, but considerable improvements needed to be done to improve the quality of the solutions.

Part V

Discussion:

Simplifying Solution Space

1 Summary of Studies

The dissertation aims to answer how solution space can be simplified to enable non-expert users to innovate and design. The overall objective was to explore the solution space in the context of user innovation related to 3D printing and to identify mechanisms in 1) the use of solution space, in 2) the structure of toolkit solution space that enables non-expert users and to 3) design new mechanisms based on the learnings of the exploration. *Part V* is the concluding Part of the dissertation and begins with a summary of the studies in the previous Parts. A discussion of the contributions and managerial implications follows next. Future research directions based on the three studies follows next along with the conclusion.

Solution space and associated toolkits for user innovation and design are the objects of study of this dissertation. After an introduction to the dissertation and explaining its challenges and outlining the definitions in *Part I,* the three studies begin. As this topic primarily deals with artifacts, the overall research approach of the dissertation was to address this topic from three perspectives, which formed its three studies. The first study, *Part II* took the point of view of the outer environment in which toolkit solution space operate. It used two exploratory sub-studies to investigate user innovators using 3D printing and related technologies. Part *III* took the perspective of the inner environment of toolkit solution space, i.e., the structure of the toolkit solution space. It explored 68 toolkits in 3D printing and analyzed the structure of their solution space. The third study in *Part IV* used the findings from *Part II* and *Part III* and followed a design science approach to design a new toolkit and evaluated it with experiments among potentials users, thereby taking the perspective of the junction of the inner and outer environments of toolkit solution space. Figure 34 depicts *Part V* in the overall research approach. The summarized Parts are below.

Part I explained user innovation regarding need information and solution information and the role of toolkits in reducing the interaction costs between manufacturers and users. The challenge of developing toolkit solution space was described, in the context of new technologies like 3D printing which potentially give a large solution space to users. The importance of developing solution space and democratizing its development for non-expert users was highlighted in existing literature leading to the research gap and identifying the overall research question of the study. The research question and its three sub-research questions where stated and

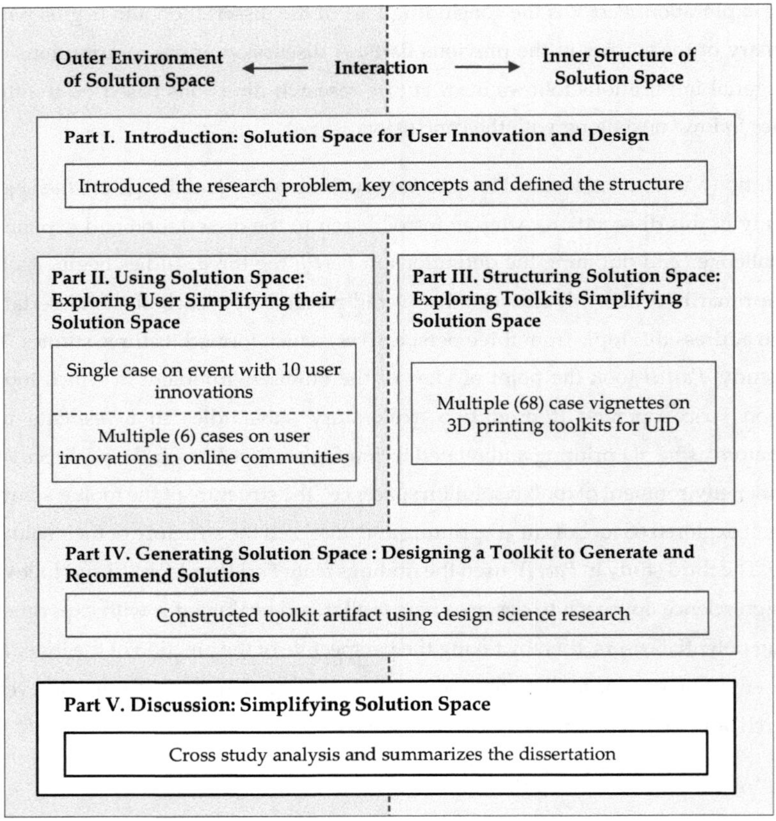

Figure 34: Overall Research Approach of Thesis

objectives defined. The theoretical framing of the dissertation followed with definitions of key terms to set the foundation for the rest of the dissertation.

1.1 Summary of Part II

Part II focused on the concept of solution space for innovation and design that a user has and its simplification by users in the context of 3D printing. It used two sub-studies that explored how users simplified solution space when creating innovative solutions. It studied user innovations in an event where users created innovative IoT products and user innovations in online communities to identified mechanisms followed by users to simplify solution space.

The first sub-study was a single case study on an offline maker event themed on the Internet of Things. The single case study contributed to understanding collaboration between participants and the design of their artifacts. The second sub-study was a multiple case study on six user innovations selected from online communities Thingiverse and Instructables. It led to the identification of the motivation of the user innovators, the role of communities involved, the role of 3D printing and other hardware toolkits, the design of their innovative artifacts and how they are published and shared among the community.

The two sub-studies developed the four stages of user innovation in making innovative products. These were 1) building minimum functionality 2) building other operational functionalities 3) optimizing design and reducing wastage and 4) integration of production. It led to the identified mechanism of initiating with toolkits that have minimum necessary solution space, before progressing to more advanced toolkits that may apply to non-users. Users also leaned towards using existing products and embedding their existing design into their products using dynamically created interfaces. It was possible by using 3D printing and low-cost computing as dynamically programmable hard and soft links respectively. Table 20 summarizes the study of *Part II*.

Table 17: Summary of Part II of the dissertation

Part II- Usage of Solution Space: Exploring User Innovations related to 3D printing	
Needs	An in-depth understanding of the use of toolkit solution space when developing innovative artifacts to identify mechanisms to simplify solution space
Challenge	Comprehensive understanding requires an understanding in the fields of user behavior, community platforms, as well as software and hardware design.
Domain	User innovators
Research Question	How do users simplify their solution space when creating innovative products?
Theoretical Lens	Modularity Theory, both in organization of the design process as well as in the design of the artifacts
Research Method	Two sub-studies: A broader multiple case study and a single case study
Data Sample	Six cases on user innovators and their user innovations out of online open source maker communities Single case of an offline maker event on internet of things
Findings	Users simplified their solution space by sharing design process among other users Users simplified their solution space by reusing design in the form of existing products and modular design Users simplified their solution space by working with the minimum necessary solution space and progressing to advanced solution space Users simplified solution space by designing dynamic interfaces between existing products with 3D printing and low-cost computing
Implications	User innovation and design in this context can be promoted for non-expert users by facilitating communities and reusing design Products can be designed to promote user innovation by offering multi-purpose interfaces
Future Research	Validate the mechanisms identified Compare the user innovation process in making products to other scenarios Design a system that creates dynamic interfaces between products
Link to Other Studies	Some of the mechanisms identified are used as starting points for Part IV

1.2 Summary of Part III

Part III narrowed down the focus from the solution space of the user to the solution space of the toolkits and analyzed the structure of toolkit solution space for mechanisms to simplify it for non-expert users. The study first identified 118 instances of 3D design software, and systematically analyzed them to shortlist a sample of 68 toolkits in 3D printing. These toolkits were further investigated using a theoretical underpinning of modularity-in-use and modularity-in-design.

This led to a categorization of toolkit solution space by the different types of design questions and design options they offer to users or the modularity-in-use of their solution space. The categorization and modularity-in-design led to the identification of four mechanisms to simplify solution space in toolkits. Mechanisms were identified by checking if they reduced design questions or/and options for the user by sharing them with other entities.

The four mechanisms identified were: 1) Offering iterative known design questions and options to users, 2) using generative algorithms to automate some of the design steps and thereby reduce design questions and options, 3) allowing users to reuse existing 2D or 3D designs, and 4) offering meta-toolkits that allow users to create their toolkits and define their solution spaces. The design of these meta-toolkits was explained in further detail. Users create their toolkits and define the design rules by which solution space is shared with each other.

The four mechanisms were presented as propositions and were design recommendations for toolkits. Some of the mechanisms identified were used as starting points for *Part IV*. Future studies can validate these mechanisms and compare with mechanisms identified in other contexts. Table 18 summarizes the study of *Part III*.

Table 18: Summary of Part III of the dissertation

Part III- Structure of Solution Space: Exploring Toolkits in 3D printing	
Need	A comprehensive understanding of the structure of toolkit solution space in 3D printing to identify existing mechanisms of simplifying solution space for non-expert users
Challenge	Solution space needs to be understood for both toolkits for user innovation and customization holistically in the context of 3D printing before mechanisms for simplifying solution space can be identified
Domain	Toolkits design
Research Question	How do toolkits for user innovation and design simplify solution space?
Theoretical Lens	Modularity-in-use which is detailed by theory on design space analysis and modularity-in-design
Research Method	Case study method with case vignettes and cross-case analysis for systemization
Data Sample	68 (out of 118) toolkits in 3D printing in the form of case vignettes
Findings	Categorization of toolkit solution space based on the design questions and options offered to users Four mechanisms to simplify solution space - offering iterative known design questions and options to users -using generative algorithms to automate some design steps -allow users to extend existing designs -offer meta-toolkits that allow users to create their own toolkits
Implications	In-depth categorization of solution space developed Toolkits for non-expert users need to be designed following these identified mechanisms
Future Research	Validate the mechanisms identified and develop measures Compare mechanisms with other mechanisms in large solution spaces
Link to Other Studies	Some of the mechanisms identified are used as starting points for Part IV

1.3 Summary of Part IV

Part IV of the dissertation used the findings from Part II and Part III along with literature on implicit needs of users and answered the research question by designing artifacts, validating and contributing to design theories. It addresses the research question of whether a toolkit that generates recommendations can simplify solution space and enable non-expert users.

This study used additional technical underpinning of recommender systems, followed design science research, and designed a toolkit for building cabinets that generated solutions and recommended them to users. The generated and recommended solutions depend on users' explicit needs as well as implicit needs detected from their choice of the solution closest to their needs. The artifacts were designed through numerous iterations of evaluation in its environment following rigorous theory.

Three artifacts were developed and presented, which together formed the toolkit (FIRST) that automates solution space for users. These artifacts are 1) a web interface for communicating needs and visualizing solutions in 3D, 2) an underlying ontology for needs-based recommendations and 3) an algorithm for solution generation and reduction. The toolkit was compared with a traditional configurator toolkit for cabinets using three experiments followed by discussion workshops.

The evaluations showed that the designed toolkit found solutions for users faster than the traditional toolkit. It showed favorable results for non-expert users with implicit or unknown needs while users with clearly specified needs preferred the traditional toolkit.

Table 19: Summary of Part IV of the dissertation

Part IV- Generating Solution Space: Designing a Toolkit to Generate and Recommend Solutions

Need	Simplify solution space for Non-expert users by automating some design steps
Challenge	While Non-expert users need assistance in developing solution information, they also need assistance in identifying their needs, i.e. developing their need information
Domain	Interaction between users and toolkits
Research Question	Can a toolkit that generates recommendations simplify solution space and enable non-expert users?
Theoretical Lens	Modularity theory from previous studies and theory on recommender systems
Research Method	Design Science Research Method
Design Context	Customizable cabinets designed in 3D
Findings	Three artifacts that make up the toolkit for designing cabinets - web interface for communicating needs and visualizing in 3D - underlying ontology for needs-based recommendations - algorithm for solution generation and reduction Evaluations based on experiments and workshops
Implications	Non-expert users with unclear needs can benefit from such a toolkit, but it also needs to allow other users to state their needs and design solutions explicitly.
Future Research	Increasing the size of experiments to avoid carry-over effects Demonstrate and evaluate the toolkit for other contexts (e.g. IoT electronics)
Link to Other Studies	The toolkit is designed based on the findings in *Part II* and *Part III*

Part V summarizes the contributions of the dissertation, provides implications to practice concerning the design of toolkit solution space and for managers using toolkits. It concludes with possible directions for future research.

2 Theoretical Contributions

This chapter integrates the theoretical contributions of the three studies that were summarized in the previous chapter. It consists of two sections. The first section presents once again, theoretical contributions from each from the three studies and the second section presents theoretical contributions that emerged from conducting cross-study analysis on the results from the three studies.

2.1 Summarized Theoretical Contributions

This section presents the theoretical contributions of the three studies and ties them against the summarized findings of each study. The classification of theory in information systems of Gregor (2006) is used to organize the contributions.

2.1.1 Theoretical Contributions of Part II

The first study, which forms *Part II* of the dissertation, explored how users simplify solution space to innovate with the theoretical lens of modularity in the organization and product design. Users simplified their solution space by specializing in certain aspects of the design and sharing the design process among other users as is seen in a more formal manner in modular organizations (Schilling, 2000). Firms have established user communities in computer games, another scenario where there can be a potentially large solution space and found that users support each other to gain solution space knowledge (L. B. Jeppesen, 2005; Prügl & Schreier, 2006). Users also exhibit this in this study, where they are not limited to a single firm or toolkit.

Users also simplified their solution space by reusing existing designs. The resulting innovative products are modular, but the modularity-in-design emerged through bottom-up integration rather than top-down system design (Baldwin & Clark, 2001). These descriptive contributions led to two design recommendations. Users followed a learning-by-doing process to innovate and design (von Hippel, 2001) that extended beyond toolkits. At first, they developed using smaller solution spaces to develop minimum functionalities they needed and over a period, increased the size of the solution space to develop better designs. A gradually increasing solution space following a satisficing to maximizing approach (Simon, 1956) is the first design recommendation for toolkits aimed at non-expert users. The second design recommendation is to enable toolkits with the creation of dynamic interfaces for integrating different systems, by combining splitting, augmentation and linking operators (Baldwin & Clark, 2001). While similar to the concept of 'systems integrators' (Brusoni & Prencipe, 2001), the dynamic interfaces in this study are developed in the decentralized and ad-hoc approach followed by user innovations in the maker context. Table 20 summarizes the findings and theoretical contributions of *Part II*.

Table 20: Findings and theoretical contributions for Part II

Findings	***Theoretical Contributions***	***Type* (Gregor, 2006)**
Users simplified their solution space by sharing design process among other users	Corroborates with previous research on user communities assisting toolkit use in computer games (L. Jeppesen, 2003; Prügl & Schreier, 2006) Observes theory on modular organizations is among users (Schilling, 2000)	Analysis and description
Users simplified their solution space by reusing design in the form of existing products and modular design	Observes emergent or unplanned modularity-in-design is in user innovation (Baldwin & Clark, 2001)	Analysis and description
Users simplified their solution space by working with the minimum necessary solution space and progressing to advanced solution space	Suggests that users innovate and design following a learning-by-doing process (von Hippel, 2001). They need toolkits that start with satisficing their needs and gradually maximizing them (Simon, 1956).	Design and Action
Users simplified solution space by designing dynamic interfaces between existing products with 3D printing and low-cost computing	Suggests that toolkits should enable creation of dynamic interfaces for integrating different systems, by combining splitting, augmentation and linking operators (Baldwin & Clark, 2001)	Design and Action

2.1.2 Theoretical Contributions of Part III

The second study, which forms *Part III* of the dissertation, explored how toolkits simplify solution space to enable non-expert users with the principles of modularity-in-use and modularity-in-design. The first contribution of the study is the 2x2-matrix framework for classifying solution space based on design questions and options. It provides further depth to the existing classification of large and small solution spaces through measures to compare solution spaces (Franke & Schreier, 2002). The categorization also identifies that iterative design questions create new solution information, while non-iterative design questions select from existing solution information.

Table 21: Findings and theoretical contributions for Part III

Findings	***Theoretical Contributions***	***Type* (Gregor, 2006)**
Categorization of toolkit solution space based on the design questions and options offered to users	The categorization provides further depth to the existing categorization of large and small solution spaces (Franke & Schreier, 2002)	Analysis
Toolkits simplified solution space by offering iterative known design questions and options to users	Suggests how toolkits can better enable non-expert users to start learning-by-doing (von Hippel, 2001).	Design and Action
Toolkits simplified solution space by using generative algorithms to automate some design steps	Suggests toolkits have algorithms to support user decision making (Gero, 1996) and automate some design decisions	Design and Action
Toolkits simplified solution space by allowing users to extend existing designs	Suggests that toolkits should share designs between users as seen in mobile (Piller et al., 2004) and computer games (L. B. Jeppesen, 2005; Prügl & Schreier, 2006)	Design and Action
Toolkits simplified solution space by offer meta-toolkits that allow users to create their toolkits	Suggests that toolkits should enable users to design their toolkits so expert users can support non-expert users.	Design and Action

The study also has four suggestions for toolkit design in the form of propositions. The first proposition suggests that iterative use of known design questions and options improves the learning-by-doing process of a toolkit for non-expert users. The second proposition states that toolkits with generative algorithms can simplify solution space by supporting users' decision making (Gero, 1996) and automate design decisions. The third proposition suggests that toolkits with features for sharing designs between users (such as online design databases) simplify solution space for users. Toolkits in other digital products such as mobiles (Piller et al., 2004) and computer games (L. B. Jeppesen, 2005; Prügl & Schreier, 2006) also follow this approach. The fourth proposition states that toolkits that allow users to create their own toolkits in the form of meta-toolkits can simplify solution space. It allows expert users to define solution space and hence the design rules under which non-expert users can operate, in the process, opening solution space development (Helminen et al., 2015). Table 21 summarizes the findings and theoretical contributions of *Part II.*

2.1.3 Theoretical Contributions of Part IV

Table 22: Findings and theoretical contributions for Part IV

Findings	**Theoretical Contributions**	**Type (Gregor, 2006)**
Designed web interface for communicating needs and visualizing in 3D	The web interface artifact can be used to describe future interfaces for toolkits which rely on visual feedback	Design and Action
Designed underlying ontology for needs-based recommendations	The ontology artifact provides a structure for representing modular products in information systems	Design and Action
Designed algorithm for solution generation and reduction	The algorithm artifact can be used to design solution generation and recommendation systems	Design and Action
Users can find solutions faster with toolkits that generated and recommended solutions than traditional toolkits.	Supports the proposition that toolkits with generative algorithms can simplify solution space for non-expert users	Prediction
Users do not necessarily find better solutions with toolkits that generate and recommend solutions provided than traditional toolkits.	Supports the proposition that toolkits with generative algorithms can simplify solution space only for non-expert users with implicit needs (von Hippel & von Krogh, 2013)	Prediction

The third study, which forms *Part IV* of the dissertation, followed a design science approach and investigated if a toolkit that generates recommendations can simplify solution space and enable non-expert users. The study used modularity as the theoretical lens and recommender systems as the technical foundation to design a toolkit (FIRST) for customizing cabinets and evaluated it with experiments. The experiments compared the newly designed toolkit against an existing toolkit design. The three artifacts that make up FIRST lies between exaptation and Invention in the DSR knowledge contribution framework (Gregor & Hevner, 2013). The web interfaces use known web technologies for 3D rendering and recommender systems are established solutions. However, the algorithm for generating solutions and the ontology are relatively new solutions. The application domain for the three artifacts is new, as toolkits have not addressed the problem of users with implicit needs in the past. Evaluating the artifacts show that while toolkits that generate and recommend solutions can help non-expert users find solutions faster, users with specific needs (that are not implicit) are not satisfied.

2.2 Cross Study Contributions

This section presents the cross-study contributions from the summarized findings above and contributions of the three studies. The first cross-study contributions are the mechanisms identified in the three studies. The second is emergent, bottom-up modularity. A unified model for simplifying solution space for user innovation and design follows next, which applies to both the user and toolkit level.

2.2.1 Mechanisms for Simplifying Solution Space

The final cross-study theoretical contribution is the set of mechanisms identified for simplifying solution space for user innovation and design through the perspective of modularity. The different perspectives taken in the three studies reveal a set of mechanisms appropriate for the non-expert users over a continuum of a single toolkit solution space to a much larger set of solution spaces to which a user may have access. Table 23 presents these mechanisms in a summarized form.

Table 23: Summarizing mechanisms for simplifying solution space

Mechanism	Effect	Level	Found in
Sharing development process with other users	Reducing solution space needed for non-expert users	User	*Part II*
Building minimum solutions with minimum necessary solution spaces	Reduces learning curve in innovating with large solution spaces	User	*Part II*
Using solution space to build interfaces instead of products	Reuse existing design in the form of existing products	User	*Part II*
Toolkits with a small set of iterative design questions and options	Reduces learning curve in using a toolkit	Toolkit	*Part III*
Toolkits with design libraries to modify and share designs	Reuse existing digital designs	Toolkit	*Part III*
Meta-toolkits for user created toolkits	Non-expert users can collaborate with expert users	Toolkit	*Part III*
Algorithms to generate designs	Users get complex designs with minimal design decisions	Toolkit	*Part III*
Generating and recommending finished solutions to users	Non-expert users find solutions that match implicit needs	User/Toolkit	*Part IV*

2.2.2 Bottom-up Modularity for User Innovation

The first two studies, show the emergence of bottom-up modularity for user innovation that follows a more democratic approach as in open source communities (Von Hippel & Von Krogh, 2006). While communities were often domain specific in the past, such as extreme sports (Franke & Shah, 2003) or computer games (L. B. Jeppesen, 2005; Prügl & Schreier, 2006), communities have formed around technologies like low cost micro-controllers or 3D printing, with a broad range of applications from designing toys to smart home products. In the context of user innovation to make tangible objects, communities like Thingiverse have emerged around technologies rather than the domain of use. In this regard, users have access to a wide variety of toolkits, often freely accessible and with varying solution spaces. They take the assistance of a variety of online support material in the form of freely available community discussions, tutorials, and designs.

The capability of creating dynamic interfaces between existing products drives bottom up modularity as users reuse their embedded designs. These interfaces can be hard interfaces printed out of 3D design files or soft interfaces that are programs running on low-cost microcontrollers or other embedded systems. Thus, using dynamic interfaces, modularity is not constrained to the boundaries of a given system.

Reusing 3D designs with toolkits that are connected to a publicly accessible design database do not need specialized interfaces, but expert users can set up design rules so that non-expert users can easily design. It leads to in meta-toolkits, which in turn result in toolkits with far fewer design questions and options for non-expert users.

2.2.3 Model for Simplifying Solution Space

The theoretical combinations that replicate across the three studies are combined to create a unified model for simplifying solution space. Figure 35 represents the model for simplifying solution space that combines the three studies. The top side of the figure shows user innovation and design in toolkits. As users with sticky need information use toolkits to create their solutions, the figure shows it as a combination of need information and solution information, which comes from users. Solution information is the result of iterative design questions and options.

The simplified solution space is shown at the bottom of the figure, again as a combination of need and solution information. However, solution space is simplified by using existing solution information as much as possible. Doing so reduces the iterative design questions and options that a user has needs to answer. The iterative design decisions that users still make can be further reduced to a minimum or better still automated by the toolkit. It changes the role of the user considerably. While the user in the past used to identify need information and develop solution information with the toolkit, the user now only identifies need information and selects finished solutions that the toolkit itself generates, possibly based on existing solutions. This simplifies solution space for the non-expert user as the user then only needs to identify need-solution pairs rather than create solutions themselves.

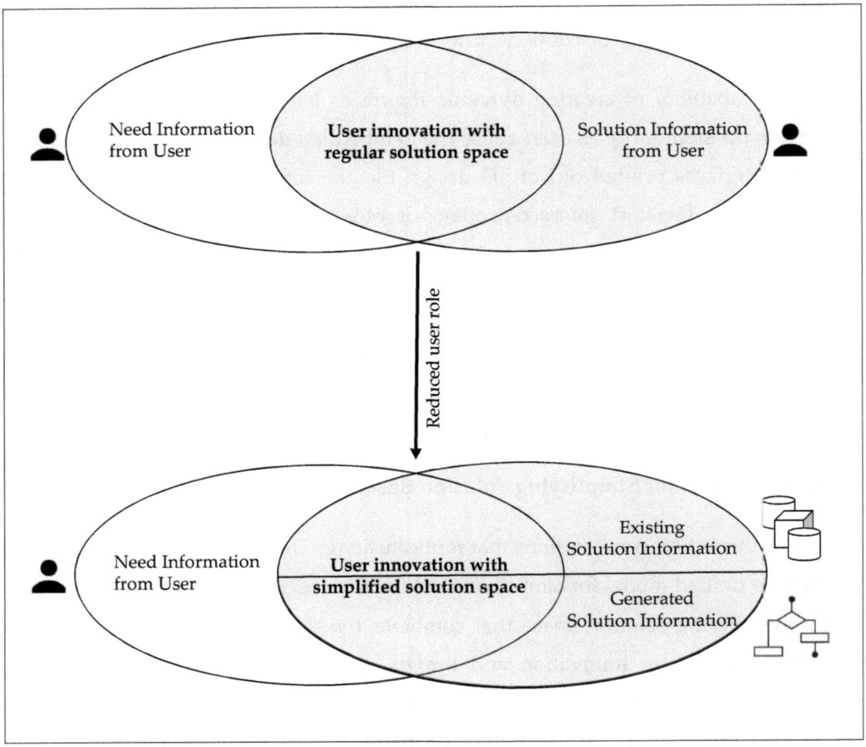

Figure 35: Model for simplifying solution space

In summary, this chapter has presented the theoretical contributions of each of the three studies of the dissertation and generated valuable cross-study theoretical contributions. The next chapter discusses implications for practice. Limitations and future research along with the conclusion come next.

3 Implications for Practice

The dissertation aims at helping both organizations and individuals better interact with each other and meet their mutual objectives of innovation and design. The dissertation meets this objective through design findings that firms can adopt in the products, services, or toolkits they offer to users and findings related to the organization between firms and users.

These implications for practice consist of three categories depending on the groups of related stakeholders they address. The first group consists of varying levels of non-expert users looking to convert their needs into solutions. The second group consists of managers of maker communities or events that revolve around toolkits and making. The third group consists of toolkit makers aiming at non-expert users and the fourth group consists of product managers aiming at expanding their markets.

The chapter describes the implications for practice in the form of answers to the following questions, which each of these groups may ask to organize themselves effectively and their design activities:

The first group that the dissertation addresses, is of non-expert users who are looking for solutions to their needs not met by standard products. A checkpoint to help these non-expert users is to ask *"What type of needs do users have?"* This question helps users understand if their needs can be explicitly stated or if they are unclear and need to be defined. If the needs can be explicitly defined, then they can look for a matching solution. Otherwise, users can evaluate a few solutions in the general area, in the process identify their needs, and find their matching solutions. The next checkpoint for non-expert users is to ask, *"What type of solutions do I require for my needs?"* Solutions for these needs can either be existing or non-existing and need to be developed. Existing solutions are already available in the market, either in the form of ready solutions or customizable solutions. Examples of such solutions are found in product catalogs, in recommender systems or configurator toolkits. Non-existing solutions can potentially be created by non-expert users, either by themselves or with the help of others. It brings us to the next question in the checklist, *"What types of toolkits provide these solutions?"* Basic toolkits such as configurators and other mass-customization toolkits provide existing solutions that may match user needs and in some cases after cycles of trial and error, provide existing solutions that match previously unidentified needs. Developing new solutions requires developing new solution information. Non-expert users can develop new solution information by the following ways. Firstly, they can develop new solutions by reducing the scope and developing minimal solutions. Secondly, they can extend existing solutions, by either using embedded solutions as building blocks or modifying existing solutions with add-ons or extensions. Thirdly, they can collaborate with other solution developers, who can be either other users or even toolkits that generate solutions.

Table 24: Questions for various stakeholder groups in practice

Stakeholder Group	Questions
Non-Expert Users	What types of needs does a user have? What types of solutions do users require for their needs? What types of toolkits provide these solutions?
Maker Community and Event Managers	What types of toolkits do community users or event participants require? What interactions need to be encouraged to support innovation activities of users?
Toolkit Makers	What functionalities should toolkits have to enable non-expert users?
Product Managers	What product modifications do lead to expansion into new markets? What product additions do lead to expansion into new markets?

Maker community and event managers can benefit from this dissertation to manage activities involving toolkits. A relevant question to them is to ask, *"What type of toolkits do community users or event participants require?"* The answer to this question depends on the profiles of members. Experts prefer the most flexibility and solution space, so they can get the exact solutions that match their exact needs. While on the other non-experts would prefer toolkits that are easy to understand but flexible enough to develop a minimum solution. Non-experts would require toolkits with varying solution spaces so that they can gradually upgrade their designs in each iteration as they develop solutions that are more advanced. Smaller maker events would not be able to provide this time for non-expert users to grow as in the case of longer run maker communities. The other question relevant to this group is to ask, *"What interactions need to be encouraged to support innovation activities of users?"* Promoting innovation activities of members who are non-experts can be done by promoting the reuse of existing solutions. Use of solution repositories and toolkits that link to external services can be encouraged. Cross-disciplinary interactions between members also promote the development of full solutions that meet real world needs.

The third group to whom the dissertation makes relevant contributions is toolkit makers asking, *"What functionalities should toolkits have to enable non-expert users?"* The mechanisms identified in *Part II* and *Part III* and designed in *Part IV* correspond to these functionalities. Toolkits that are used to design components that act as interfaces between products can focus on having prebuilt all-purpose interfaces or automatic generation of designs that are complementary to existing products. Toolkits should also offer design questions that have few design options, but can iteratively be used as building blocks to design complicated shapes. Advanced design questions can also be offered on demand to users who have gradually become more involved and comfortable with the toolkit. Reusing solution information in the toolkit is essential, and either sharing solutions can achieve it or allowing users to build their extendable solution information in the form of user-created toolkits. Furthermore, as non-expert users benefit from the availability of solutions and over time can contribute to their own solutions, users and solutions show cross-sided network effects (Eisenmann, Parker, & Van Alstyne, 2006)[26]. Hence it is in the interest of toolkit makers to take a page from community managers (Weitzel, Beimborn, & Koenig, 2006) and offer some useful solution content themselves, with a benchmarking study, comparing existing toolkits in the market. Free access to the solution information reduces barriers to reuse. Revenue sharing mechanisms can also be imbibed into the toolkit if users purchase solutions through the toolkit. Automating solution generation and evaluation can

[26] Cross-side network effects occur when usage of one product or network spawns an increase in a complimentary product or network (Eisenmann et al., 2006)

reduce many unnecessary design steps from users but reduces their feeling of ownership of the design. These methods can be used in addition to traditional toolkits to derive benefits from both approaches.

The fourth and the final group this dissertation is addressed to are product managers asking, *"What product modifications can help me expand to new markets."* Part II suggested dynamic interfaces between existing products that were not designed to connect to each other as a means of simplifying the solution space for the user to innovate. It implies that products with all-purpose interfaces, preferably those following an established industry standard can encourage non-expert user to come up with new applications of the product by combining them with other products and using them in unforeseen ways. Product firms can then acquire new applications that are popular and then include them in their product portfolio. This new offering can then be tightly integrated and produced more efficiently to capture the most value from the identified innovative combination. The other directions firms can go to is to specialize on certain components of their products and offer them as standalone products with all-purpose interfaces. An example for this is a digital lens for the smartphone provided by camera producers. Through the means of a digital interface (wireless connection) and a physical interface (adjustable clip), a camera producer can focus on offering a high-quality lens while reusing functionalities of a smartphone that a user is expected always to have. These functionalities of the smartphone such as a display, buttons, and storage are superior to that of a camera, even if the smartphone has a low-end camera itself. The camera lens allows the camera producer to compete only against the inferior lens rather than the whole smartphone, which is a bundled product.

4 Limitations and Future Research

The limitations of the three studies are necessary addendums to the contributions and implications of this dissertation. The limitations of the three studies are once again summarized, and the limitations of the dissertation as a whole are discussed. It is used further to identify avenues for future research.

4.1 Limitations of the Studies

Part II of the dissertation studied simplifying of users' solution space in the context of user innovation communities and events in making or prototyping. Open source hardware and software influences the context of this study. The underlying principles of open source software and hardware thus form a huge bias in the study. The results may not be generalizable to user innovation in firms dealing with proprietary products or to short-term innovation communities set up by companies. The context of maker communities and events is relatively new and rapidly changing. Various factors can heavily influence directions of these communities. For example, although STL files are common in the 3D printing industry and found in communities like Thingiverse, they are not as easy to modify as the native files of an expert 3D designing software. Another limitation is that most of the cases of user innovations have remained at the prototyping stage. The shift to production has been relatively rare and not exclusively studied in this study.

Part III of the dissertation studied simplifying toolkit solution space and restricted itself to toolkits for user innovation and design in 3D printing. The four mechanisms identified in this context may not be complete. The study also does not extensively include the opinions of toolkit makers (except Mixee Labs). An extensive qualitative study of the opinions of toolkit makers may provide further reasoning for the solution space structure and help in the identification of other mechanisms. The cases were also limited to publicly available 3D printing toolkits and excluded professional CAD software which may have important mechanisms for simplifying solution space that is not captured. A limitation of the meta-toolkit is that non-expert users have to depend on expert users to innovate for them while the non-expert users are restricted to customization.

As *Part IV* of the dissertation followed a design science approach, the context was set to a real world problem, which makes the underlying findings hard to generalize. Basing the design on a KRS means that the toolkit is limited by the quality of the information in the underlying knowledge base (Ricci et al., 2011). The constructed artifacts were also evaluated relatively, in comparison with another prototype toolkit. It lacked an ideal evaluation method or a comparison with a successful toolkit in production. Some of the participants also argued that the application context of the toolkit was not complex enough to require recommendation support. Along with limitations of the single study design followed in the experiments, the participants were all students within the same age group, and they were familiar with modern online applications. Their interest in using the toolkit was simulated, which makes it hard to measure the degree of satisfaction.

The dissertation overall is constrained by its theoretical focus. Simplification of solution space is interpreted regarding modularity-in-use and modularity-in-design, which is reflected in all three studies. Solution space for user innovation and design in the context of this dissertation was also restricted to digital fabrication, an area whose capabilities and limitations are rapidly changing. Based on these limitations the following avenues for future research are proposed.

4.2 Future Research

The first future research direction suggested is to replicate these studies in other areas of large and open solution spaces such as in mobile apps development or working with open data and look at interrelationships between these studies. Toolkits in mobile apps development are at a much more mature stage and may represent a future direction for all such cases.

The open user communities mentioned in *Part II* have a large user base and user participation, but tapping into it is a challenge to firms, and it needs to be further researched. Future DSR studies can look into how open user innovation communities can be used for innovation contests so that both user needs and solution information can be derived at prototype stages. As the variety and individualization of users increase with the large solution spaces, managing it also becomes a problem that design of unique artifacts can solve. Hence, a future research question in this direction can be along the lines of new service creation where companies can design new services that manage the complexity of individual products through information systems. *Part II* identified the existence of dynamic interfaces, which can be investigated further in future research. Further design aspects of these interfaces and designing a system that can create interfaces automatically without user skill would further affect user innovation in making.

The study on toolkits in *Part III* was done with the perspective of modularity, identified propositions that can be quantitatively tested. Solution space simplification here was studied from the perspective of decreasing the cost of user design to make it attractive to non-expert users. It can also be studied from the perspective of increasing the value for non-expert users that make the design effort worthwhile. It is an ideal DSR research topic, as it can leverage better needs identification and rating of these needs to provide solutions that create the most value for users.

The DSR research done in *Part IV* can be further extended by increasing the evaluation cycles and improving the design until all the proposed hypothesis get supported. The toolkit in *Part IV* was in the context of customizable cabinets. However, it can be extended to other complex contexts such as designing IoT electronics or designing complex 3D shapes.

5 Conclusion

To conclude, the dissertation answers the research question: *How can toolkit solution space be simplified to enable non-expert users for user innovation and design?* A problem that is of growing importance as the technology to prototype and cater to individual needs becomes increasingly affordable, thus beckoning a future where *all users* can develop solutions they need, solving problems only they understand. The research question was explored qualitatively from two perspectives by looking at the solution space(s) of users and the solution space of toolkits. The findings from these studies contributed to the third study, where a new toolkit was designed that generated solutions and recommended appropriate solutions to users. It can further bring down the cost of enabling non-expert users to innovate and design. In the end, the dissertation identified eight mechanisms for simplifying solution space using modularity theory as a basis.

At the user level, user innovators followed an approach of minimizing the new solution information they needed to develop by reusing existing designs and sharing solution information with other users. When they had to create new designs, they created interfaces between existing designs out of basic building blocks. Over time, users optimized their designs by creating more integrated and optimized solutions. At a toolkit level, providing existing design information in the form of basic design questions and options, reusing existing designs, taking the assistance of algorithms, and user created toolkits simplify solution space for non-expert users. Algorithms can also generate finished designs, identify user needs, and recommend matching solutions to users. This dissertation has implications for users, innovation community and event managers, toolkit makers and product managers as it takes one-step closer to democratizing innovation and design by bringing it to the masses.

References

Abernathy, W. J., & Clark, K. B. (1985). Innovation - Mapping the Winds of Creative Destruction. *Research Policy, 14*(1), 3–22.

Baafi, E., & Millner, A. (2011). A toolkit for tinkering with tangibles & connecting communities. *Proceedings of the Fifth International Conference on Tangible, Embedded, and Embodied Interaction - TEI '11*, 349.

Baldwin, C. Y., & Clark, K. (2001). *Design Rules: The Power of Modularity* (Vol. 1). MIT Press.

Baldwin, C. Y., & Clark, K. B. (2004). Modularity in the Design of Complex Engineering Systems. In *Complex Engineered Systems Understanding Complex Systems* (pp. 175–205).

Baldwin, C. Y., Hienerth, C., & von Hippel, E. (2006). How user innovations become commercial products: A theoretical investigation and case study. *Research Policy, 35*, no. 9(March), 1291–1313.

Balka, K., Raasch, C., & Herstatt, C. (2009). Open Source beyond software◎: An empirical investigation of the open design phenomenon. *R&D Management Conference*, (April), 1–28.

Balka, K., Raasch, C., & Herstatt, C. (2014). The effect of selective openness on value creation in user innovation communities. *Journal of Product Innovation Management, 31*(2), 392–407.

Bettman, J. R., Luce, M. F., & Payne, J. W. (1998). Constructive Consumer Choice Processes. *Journal of Consumer Research, 25*(3), 187–217.

Bogers, M., Afuah, A., & Bastian, B. (2010). Users as Innovators: A Review, Critique, and Future Research Directions. *Journal of Management, 36*(4), 857–875.

Briscoe, G., & Mulligan, C. (2014). Digital Innovation: The Hackathon Phenomenon. *Creativeworks London*, (6), 1–13.

Brodbeck, M., & Polanyi, M. (1960). Personal Knowledge: Towards a Post-Critical Philosophy. *American Sociological Review*.

Brody, P., & Pureswaran, V. (2013). The new software-defined supply chain: Preparing for the disruptive transformation of Electronics design and manufacturing. *IBM Institute for Business Value*, 18.

Brusoni, S., & Prencipe, A. (2001). Unpacking the black box of modularity: Technologies, products and organization. *Industrial and Corporate Change, 10*(1), 179–205.

Bull, G., & Groves, J. (2009). The Democratization of Production. *Learning & Leading with Technology, 5191*(November), 36–37.

Burke, R. (2007). Hybrid web recommender systems. In *The adaptive web* (pp. 377–408).

Chatterjee, S. (2015). Writing My next Design Science Research Masterpiece: But How Do I Make a Theoretical Contribution to DSR? *European Conference on Information Systems (ECIS)*, 0–14.

Chen, S., Wang, Y., & Tseng, M. M. (2009). Mass customisation as a collaborative engineering effort. *International Journal of Collaborative Engineering, 1*(1/2), 152.

Chesbrough, H. W. (2003). The era of open innovation. *Management Review, 44(3)*(3), 35–41.

Chorianopoulos, K., Jaccheri, L., & Nossum, A. S. (2012). Creative and open software engineering practices and tools in maker community projects. *Proceedings of the 4th ACM SIGCHI Symposium on Engineering Interactive Computing Systems - EICS '12*, 333.

Christensen, L. B. (2007). *Experimental methodology - 10th Ed.*

Clark, K. B. (1985). The interaction of design hierarchies and market concepts in technological evolution. *Research Policy, 14*(5), 235–251.

Clark, K. B., Chew, W. B., Fujimoto, T., Meyer, J., & Scherer, F. M. (1987). Product Development in the World Auto Industry. *Brookings Papers on Economic Activity, 1987*(3), 729.

Coutaz, J. (1987). PAC, an Object Oriented Model for Dialog Design. In *Human-Computer Interaction - INTERACT* (pp. 431–436).

Cvijikj, I., & Michahelles, F. (2011). The Toolkit Approach for End-user Participation in the Internet of Things. In *Architecting the Internet of Things SE - 4* (pp. 65–96).

Cyledge. (2014). Explore The World of Configurators! | Configurator Database.

De Bruyn, a., Liechty, J. C., Huizingh, E. K. R. E., & Lilien, G. L. (2008). Offering Online Recommendations with Minimum Customer Input Through Conjoint-Based Decision Aids. *Marketing Science, 27*(1), 443–460.

Dellaert, B. G. C., & Stremersch, S. (2005). Marketing Mass-Customized Products: Striking a Balance between Utility and Complexity. *Journal of Marketing Research, 42*(2), 219–227.

Dimitrov, D., Schreve, K., & Beer, N. De. (2006). Advances in three dimensional printing – state of the art and future perspectives. *Rapid Prototyping Journal, 12*(3), 136–147.

Dong, J. Q., & Wu, W. (2015). Business value of social media technologies: Evidence from online user innovation communities. *Journal of Strategic Information Systems, 24*(2), 113–127.

Dorst, K., & Cross, N. (2001). Creativity in the design process: Co-evolution of problem-solution. *Design Studies, 22*(5), 425–437.

Eisenhardt, K. M. (1989). Building theories from case study research. *Academy of Management Review, 14*(4), 532–550.

Eisenhardt, K. M. (1991). Better Stories and Better Constructs: the Case for Rigor and Comparative Logic. *Academy of Management Review, 16*(3), 620–627.

Eisenmann, T., Parker, G., & Van Alstyne, M. W. (2006). Strategies for Two-Sided Markets. *Havard Business Review, October*, 1–12.

Enos, J. L. (1962). Invention and Innovation in the Petroleum Refining Industry. *Nber, I*, 299–322.

Felfernig, A., & Burke, R. (2008). Constraint-based recommender systems: technologies and research issues. *Proceedings of the 10th International Conference on Electronic Commerce ICEC '08, 8*(5), 1–10.

Felfernig, A., Friedrich, G., & Schmidt-Thieme, L. (2007). Guest Editors' Introduction: Recommender Systems. *IEEE Intelligent Systems, 22*(3), 18–21.

Forbes. (2015). Nestle on the Forbes World's Most Valuable Brands List.

Foxall, G., & Tierney, J. (1984). From CAP 1 to CAP 2: User-Initiated Innovation from the User's Point of View. *Management Decision, 22*(5), 3–15.

Franke, N., Keinz, P., & Schreier, M. (2008). Complementing mass customization toolkits with user communities: How peer input improves customer self-design. *Journal of Product Innovation Management, 25*(6), 546–559.

Franke, N., Keinz, P., & Steger, C. J. (2009). Testing the Value of Customization: When Do Customers Really Prefer Products Tailored to Their Preferences? *Journal of Marketing, 73*(September), 103–121.

Franke, N., & Piller, F. (2003). Key research issues in user interaction with user toolkits in a mass customisation system. *International Journal of Technology Management, 26*(5–6), 578–599.

Franke, N., & Piller, F. (2004). Value Creation by Toolkits for User Innovation and Design: The Case of the Watch Market. *Journal of Product Innovation Management, 21*(6), 401–415.

Franke, N., & Schreier, M. (2002). Entrepreneurial opportunities with toolkits for user innovation and design. *International Journal on Media Management, 4*(4), 225–234.

Franke, N., & Schreier, M. (2010). Why customers value self-designed products: The importance of process effort and enjoyment. In *Journal of Product Innovation Management* (Vol. 27, pp. 1020–1031).

Franke, N., Schreier, M., & Kaiser, U. (2010). The "I Designed It Myself" Effect in Mass Customization. *Management Science, 56*(1), 125–140.

Franke, N., & Shah, S. (2003). How communities support innovative activities: an exploration of assistance and sharing among end-users. *Research Policy, 32*(1), 157–178.

Franke, N., & von Hippel, E. (2003). Satisfying heterogeneous user needs via innovation toolkits: the case of Apache security software. *Research Policy*, 1199–1215.

Freeman, C., Robertson, A. B., Whittaker, P. J., Curnow, R. C., Fuller, J. K., Hanna, S., … Fassinotti, J. L. (1968). Chemical process plant: Innovation and the world market. *National Institute Economic Review, 45*(1), 29–57.

Garud, R., & Kumaraswamy, A. (1993). Changing competitive dynamics in network industries: An exploration of Sun Microsystems' open systems strategy. *Strategic Management Journal, 14*(5), 351–369.

Genesereth, M. R., & Nilsson, N. J. (1987). Logical Foundations of Artificial Intelligence. *The Journal of Symbolic Logic*.

Gero, J. (1996). Design tools that learn: A possible CAD future. *Information Processing in Civil and Structural Design, Civil-Comp Press, Edinburgh.*

Gill, T. G., & Hevner, A. R. (2013). A Fitness-Utility Model for Design Science Research. *ACM Trans. Manage. Inf. Syst., 4*(2), 5:1–5:24.

Gilmore, J. H., & Pine, B. J. (1997). The four faces of mass customization. *Harvard Business Review, 75*(1), 91–101.

Glaser, B. G. (1965). The Constant Comparative Method of Qualitative Analysis. *Social Problems, 12*(4), 436–445.

Goduscheit, R. C., & Jørgensen, J. H. (2013). User toolkits for innovation - a literature review. *International Journal of Technology Management, 61*(3/4), 274.

Gregor, S. (2006). The Nature of Theory in Information Systems. *MIS Quarterly, 30*(3), 611–642.

Gregor, S., & Hevner, A. R. (2013). Positioning and Presenting Design Science Research for Maximum Impact. *MIS Quarterly, 37*(2), 337–355.

Grimm, T. (2004). *User's Guide to Rapid Prototyping*. Society of Manufacturing Engineers.

Gruber, T. (1995). Toward principles for the design of ontologies used for knowledge sharing. *International Journal of Human-Computer Studies, 43*(5–6), 907–928.

Harhoff, D., Henkel, J., & von Hippel, E. (2003). Profiting from voluntary information spillovers: how users benefit by freely revealing their innovations. *Research Policy, 32*(10), 1753–1769.

Helminen, P., Ainoa, J., & Mäkinen, S. (2015). Designing user innovation toolkits: exploring the interrelation between solution space and module library. *International Journal of Design Creativity and Innovation*, (May), 1–19.

Hermans, G. (2012). A model for evaluating the solution space of mass customization toolkits. *International Journal of Industrial Engineering and Management, 3*(4), 205–214.

Hermans, G. (2014). Investigating the Unexplored Possibilities of Digital-Physical Toolkits in Lay Design. *International Journal of Design, 8*(2), 15–28.

Herstatt, C., & von Hippel, E. (1992). From experience: Developing new product concepts via the lead user method: A case study in a "low-tech" field. *Journal of Product Innovation Management, 9*(3), 213–221.

Hevner, A. R., March, S. T. S., Park, J., & Ram, S. (2004). Design science in information systems research. *MIS Quarterly, 28*(1), 75–105.

Honey, M. ., & Kanter, D. E. . (2013). *Design, make, play: Growing the next generation of STEM innovators. Routledge.*

Huffman, C., & Kahn, B. (1998). Variety for sale: mass customization or mass confusion? *Journal of Retailing, 74*(302), 491–513.

Hung, C.-L., Chou, J. C.-L., & Dong, T.-P. (2011). Innovations and communication through innovative users: An exploratory mechanism of social networking website. *International Journal of Information Management, 31*(4), 317–326.

Jannach, D., Zanker, M., Ge, M., & Gröning, M. (2012). Recommender Systems in Computer Science and Information Systems–A Landscape of Research. In *E-Commerce and Web Technologies* (pp. 76–87).

Jeppesen, L. (2003). the Implications of "User Toolkits for Innovation." *DRUID Summer Conference 2003 on Creating, Sharing and Transferring Knowledge.*, 1–31.

Jeppesen, L. B. (2005). User toolkits for innovation: Consumers support each other. *Journal of Product Innovation Management, 22*, 347–362.

Jeppesen, L. B., & Frederiksen, L. (2006). Why Do Users Contribute to Firm-Hosted User Communities? The Case of Computer-Controlled Music Instruments. *Organization Science, 17*(July 2015), 45–63.

Jeppesen, L. B., & Molin, M. J. (2003). Consumers as Co-developers: Learning and Innovation Outside the Firm. *Technology Analysis & Strategic Management, 15*, 363–383.

Kambil, A., Friesen, G. B., & Sundaram, A. (1999). Co-creation: A new source of value. *Outlook Journal*, (2), 38–43.

Kankanhalli, A., Ye, H., & Teo, H. (2015). Comparing Potential and Actual Innovators: An Empirical Study of Mobile Data Services Innovation. *MIS Quarterly, 39*(3), 667–682.

Kohler, T., Fueller, J., Stieger, D., & Matzler, K. (2011). Avatar-based innovation: Consequences of the virtual co-creation experience. *Computers in Human Behavior, 27*(1), 160–168.

Kohler, T., Matzler, K., & Füller, J. (2009). Avatar-based innovation: Using virtual worlds for real-world innovation. *Technovation, 29*(6–7), 395–407.

Krumholz, H. M., Curry, L. A., & Bradley, E. H. (2011). Survival after acute myocardial infarction (SAMI) study: the design and implementation of a positive deviance study. *American Heart Journal, 162*(6), 981–987.e9.

Kujala, S. (2002). *User studies: a practical approach to user involvement for gathering user needs and requirements* (Vol. 1).

Kyriakou, H., Englehardt, S., & Nickerson, J. V. (2012). Networks of Innovation in 3d Printing. *SSRN Electronic Journal.*

Lakhani, K. R., & Von Hippel, E. (2003). How open source software works: "free" user-to-user assistance. *Research Policy, 32*(6), 923–943.

Lee, K. (1996). The role of user firms in the innovation of machine tools: The Japanese case. *Research Policy, 25*, 491–507.

Leff, A., & Rayfield, J. T. (2001). Web-application development using the Model/View/Controller design pattern. In *Proceedings - 5th IEEE International Enterprise Distributed Object Computing Conference* (Vol. 2001–Janua, pp. 118–127).

Li, M., Kankanhalli, A., & Kim, S. H. (2016). Which ideas are more likely to be implemented in online user innovation communities? An empirical analysis. *Decision Support Systems, 84*, 28–40.

Lüthje, C. (2004). Characteristics of innovating users in a consumer goods field. *Technovation, 24*(9), 683–695.

Lüthje, C., Herstatt, C., & von Hippel, E. (2005). User-innovators and "local" information: The case of mountain biking. *Research Policy*, 1–29.

MacLean, A., Young, R., Bellotti, V., & Moran, T. (1991). Questions, Options, and Criteria: Elements of Design Space Analysis. *Human-Computer Interaction, 6*(3), 201–250.

Mahr, D., & Lievens, A. (2012). Virtual lead user communities: Drivers of knowledge creation for innovation. *Research Policy, 41*(1), 167–177.

Maranville, S. (1992). Entrepreneurship in the business curriculum. *Journal of Education for Business, 68*(1), 27.

Matzler, K., Waiguny, M., & Füller, J. (2007). Spoiled for Choice®: Consumer Confusion in Internet-Based Mass Customization. *Innovative Marketing, 3*(3), 7–18.

Mikhak, B., Lyon, C., & Gorton, T. M. (2003). The Tower system: A toolkit for prototyping tangible user interfaces. *Submitted as a Long Paper to CHI*, (September), 1–8.

Mitchell, V.-W., & Papavassiliou, V. (1999). Marketing causes and implications of consumer confusion. *Journal of Product & Brand Management, 8*(4), 319–342.

Naik, H. S. (2013). Dissertation Proposal: Towards User Co-created Toolkits. In *International Conference on Information Systems: Reshaping Society Through Information Systems Design*. Bocconi University, Milan, Italy.

Naik, H. S., & Möslein, K. M. (2013). Towards User Created Toolkits. In *Open and User Innovation Conference*. CENTRIM, Brighton Business School, University of Brighton.

Naik, H. S., & Möslein, K. M. (2014). Dynamic Interfaces for User Innovation. In *Open and User Innovation Conference*. Harvard Business School, Boston, MA.

Naik, H. S., Velamuri, V. K., & Möslein, K. M. (2016). Simplifying Solution Space: A multiple case study on 3D printing toolkits. In *European Conference on Information Systems*. Istanbul, Turkey.

Ogawa, S. (1998). Does sticky information affect the locus of innovation? Evidence from the Japanese convenience-store industry. *Research Policy, 26*(7–8), 777–790.

Oliveira, P., & von Hippel, E. (2011). Users as service innovators: The case of banking services. *Research Policy, 40*(6), 806–818.

Orton, D. J., & Weick, K. E. (1990). Systems®: Coupled Loosely A Reconceptualization The University of Michigan. *Academy of Management Review, 15*(2), 203–223.

Pearce, J. M. (2012). Materials science. Building research equipment with free, open-source hardware. *Science (New York, N.Y.), 337*(6100), 1303–4.

Peffers, K., & Tuunanen, T. (2007). A design science research methodology for information systems research. *Journal of Management …, 24*(3), 45–77.

Piller, F. (2005). Mass Customization®: Reflections on the State of the Concept. *International Journal of Flexible Manufacturing Systems, 16*(4), 313–334.

Piller, F., Ihl, C., Füller, J., Stotko, C., & Ag, C. E. O. H. (2004). Toolkits for Open Innovation - The Case of Mobile Phone Games. *Proceedings of the 37th Hawaii International Conference on System Sciences, 0*(C), 1–10.

Piller, F., Ihl, C., Vossen, A., & Group, I. M. (2011). A Typology of Customer Co-creation in the Innovation Process. *New Forms of Collaborative Production and Innovation: Economic, Social, Legal and Technical Characteristics and Conditions*, 31–61.

Piller, F., Schubert, P., Koch, M., & Möslein, K. (2005). Overcoming Mass Confusion: Collaborative Customer Co-Design in Online Communities. *Journal of Computer-Mediated Communication, 10*(4), 00–00.

Piller, F., & Walcher, D. (2006). Toolkits for idea competitions: a novel method to integrate users in new product development. *R and D Management, 36*(3), 307–318.

Prahalad, C. K., & Ramaswamy, V. (2004). Co-creation experiences: The next practice in value creation. *Journal of Interactive Marketing, 18*(3), 5–14.

Prügl, R., & Schreier, M. (2006). Learning from leading-edge customers at the Sims: Opening up the innovation process using toolkits. *R and D Management, 36*(3), 237–250.

Raasch, C., Herstatt, C., & Balka, K. (2009). On the open design of tangible goods. *R and D Management, 39*(4), 382–393.

Raasch, C., Herstatt, C., & Lock, P. (2008). The Dynamics of User Innovation: Drivers and Impediments of Innovation Activities. *International Journal of Innovation Management, 12*(3), 377–398.

Randall, T., Terwiesch, C., & Ulrich, K. (2007). Research Note—User Design of Customized Products. *Marketing Science, 26*(2), 268–280.

Randall, T., Terwiesch, C., & Ulrich, K. T. (2005). Principles for User Design of Customized Products. *California Management Review, 47*(4), 68–85.

Resnick, P., & Varian, H. R. (1997). Recommender systems. *Communications of the ACM, 40*(3), 56–58.

Ricci, F., Rokach, L., & Shapira, B. (2011). Introduction to Recommender Systems Handbook. In *Recommender Systems Handbook* (pp. 1–35).

Rittel, H. J., & Webber, M. M. (1984). Planning problems are wicked problems. In *Developments in Design Methodology* (pp. 135–144).

Roy, R. (2009). New market emergence and the product strategies of de novo and de alio entrants in the industrial robotics industry. In *Atlanta Competitive Advantage Conference*.

Runeson, P., & Höst, M. (2008). Guidelines for conducting and reporting case study research in software engineering. *Empirical Software Engineering, 14*(2), 131–164.

Sahaym, A., Steensma, H. K., & Schilling, M. A. (2007). The Influence of Information Technology on the Use of Loosely Coupled Organizational Forms: An Industry-Level Analysis. *Organization Science, 18*(5), 865–880.

Salvador, F., & Forza, C. (2004). Key principles for sales configuration design. In *International Conference on Economic, Technical and Organisational aspects of Product Configuration Systems (PETO) 2004*.

Salvador, F., Holan, P. De, & Piller, F. (2009). Cracking the code of mass customization. *MIT Sloan Management Review, 50*(50315), 71.

Sanchez, R., & Mahoney, J. T. (1996). Modularity, flexibility, and knowledge management in product and organization design. *Strategic Management Journal, 17*(S2), 63–76.

Schilling, M. A. (2000). Toward a general modular systems theory and its application to interfirm product modularity. *Academy of Management Review, 25*(2), 312–334.

Schilling, M. A., & Steensma, H. K. (2001). The use of modular organizational forms: An industry-level analysis. *Academy of Management Journal, 44*(6), 1149–1168.

Scott, J. (2000). Understanding Contemporary Society: Theories of The Present - Rational Choice theory. In *The British journal of sociology* (Vol. 50, pp. 671–85).

Sheridan, K. M., Halverson, E. R., Litts, B. K., Brahms, L., Jacobs-Priebe, L., & Owens, T. (2014). Learning in the Making: A Comparative Case Study of Three Makerspaces. *Harvard Educational Review, 84*(4), 505-531-565.

Simon, H. A. (1955). A Behavioral Model of Rational Choice. *The Quarterly Journal of Economics, 69*(1), 99–118.

Simon, H. A. (1956). Rational choice and the structure of the environment. *Psychological Review, 63*(2), 129–138.

Simon, H. A. (1969). *The Sciences of the Artificial. Cambridge, MA* (Vol. 1).

Simon, H. A. (1973). The Structure of Ill Structured Problems. *Artificial Intelligence, 4*(3–4), 181–201.

Sitthi-amorn, P., Lan, J., & Wang, W. (2015). MultiFab®: A Machine Vision Assisted Platform for Multi-material 3D Printing. *ACM Transactions on Graphics,* (34), 11.

Slaughter, S. (1993). Innovation and learning during implementation: a comparison of user and manufacturer innovations. *Research Policy,* 22(1), 81–95.

Slovic, P. (1995). The construction of preference. *American Psychologist, 50*(5), 364–371.

Smith, B. (2003). Ontology. *Blackwell Guide to the Philosophy of Computing and Information,* (1964), 155–166.

Snyder, R. (2014). An overview of the past, present, and future of 3D printing technology with an emphasis on the present. *Association Supporting Computer Users in Education " ....*

Stava, O., Vanek, J., Benes, B., Carr, N., & Měch, R. (2012). Stress Relief: Improving Structural Strength of 3D Printable Objects. *ACM Transactions on Graphics, 31*(4), 1–11.

Syam, N., Krishnamurthy, P., & Hess, J. D. (2008). That's What I Thought I Wanted? Miswanting and Regret for a Standard Good in a Mass-Customized World. *Marketing Science,* 27(3), 379–397.

Sydow, S. L. (2015). The organization of personal fabrication - Hackathons and makerspaces as semi-professional places for creative making. In *Critical*

Alternatives. Aarhus.

Teresko, J. (1994). Mass Customization or Mass Confusion? *Industry Week, 12*, 45–48.

Thomas Kohler, Johann Fueller, Kurt Matzler, & Daniel Stieger. (2011). Co-Creation In Virtual Worlds: The Design Of The User Experience. *MIS Quarterly, 35*(3), 773–788.

Thomke, S., & Von Hippel, E. (2002). Customer as Innovators: A New Way to Create Value. *Harvard Business Review, 80*, 74–81.

Tietz, R., Morrison, P. D., Luthje, C., & Herstatt, C. (2005). The process of user-innovation: a case study in a consumer goods setting. *International Journal of Product Development, 2*(4), 321–338.

Trentin, A., Perin, E., & Forza, C. (2013). Sales configurator capabilities to avoid the product variety paradox: Construct development and validation. *Computers in Industry, 64*, 436–447.

Tseng, M., & Jiao, J. (1996). Design for Mass Customization. *Annals of the CIRP, 45*(1), 153–156.

Ulrich, K. (1995). The role of product architecture in the manufacturing firm. *Research Policy, 24*(3), 419–440.

Urban, G. L., & von Hippel, E. (1988). Lead User Analyses for the Development of New Industrial Products. *Management Science, 34*(5), 569–582.

von Hippel, E. (1976). The dominant role of users in the scientific instrument innovation process. *Research Policy*.

von Hippel, E. (1977). The dominant role of the user in semiconductor and electronic subassembly process innovation. *Engineering Management, IEEE Transactions ...*.

von Hippel, E. (1978a). A customer-active paradigm for industrial product idea generation. *Research Policy, 7*(3), 240–266.

von Hippel, E. (1978b). Successful industrial products from customer ideas. *The Journal of Marketing*.

von Hippel, E. (1986). Lead Users: A Source of Novel Product Concepts. *Management Science, 32*(7), 791–805.

von Hippel, E. (1994). "Sticky information" and the locus of problem solving: implications for innovation. *Management Science*, 1–19.

von Hippel, E. (2001). PERSPECTIVE: User toolkits for innovation. *Journal of Product Innovation Management, 18*(4), 247–257.

von Hippel, E. (2005). *Democratizing innovation*. MIT Press.

von Hippel, E., & Finkelstein, S. N. (1979). Analysis of innovation in automated clinical chemistry analyzers. *Science and Public Policy, 6*(1), 23–37.

von Hippel, E., & Katz, R. (2002). Shifting Innovation to Users via Toolkits. *Management Science, 48*(7), 821–833.

von Hippel, E., & Riggs, W. (1996). *A lead user study of electronic home banking services: lessons from the learning curve* (No. WP 3911-96.).

von Hippel, E., & von Krogh, G. (2013). *Identifying viable "need-solution pairs": Problem solving without problem formulation. SSRN Electronic Journal.*

Von Hippel, E., & Von Krogh, G. (2006). Free revealing and the private-collective model for innovation incentives. *R and D Management, 36*(3), 295–306.

Voss, C. (1985). The Role of Users in the Development of Applications Software. *Journal of Product Innovation Management, 2*(2), 113–121.

Weaver, W. (1948). Science and complexity. *American Scientist, 36*(4), 536–544.

Weick, K. E. (1976). Educational Organizations as Loosely Coupled Systems. *Administrative Science Quarterly, 21*(1), 1.

Weitzel, T., Beimborn, D., & Koenig, W. (2006). A unified economic model of standard diffusion: The impact of standardization cost, network effects, and network topology. *MIS Quarterly, 30*, 489–514.

West, J., & Kuk, G. (2014). Proprietary Benefits from Open Communities: How MakerBot Leveraged Thingiverse in 3D Printing. *SSRN, 2544970*, 0–26.

Whitney, D. (2004). Physical limits to modularity. *Engineering Systems Symposium 2004*.

Yin, R. K. (2009). *Case Study Research: Design and Methods. Essential guide to qualitative methods in organizational research* (Vol. 5).

Zipkin, P. (1997). The limits of mass customization. *Harvard Business Review, 42*(3), 81–87.

Annexes

Annex A: Questionnaire for user innovators

- Shortly describe your intended product
  - What was the motivation behind it?
- How did you go about designing the product?
  - Specifically hardware
  - Specifically software
  - What is your contribution to the product?
- What were the factors and constraints?
  - Cost
  - Availability of components
  - Openness
  - What tools (if any) did you use for the design process and why?
- Was it developed individually or the result of contributions from a community?
  - Did this decision affect the design choices in developing the product?
- How did he involve others into the development of the product?
- Creativity process:
  - Did he know exactly what he wanted to develop?
  - Did the idea of the product change during the design process?
  - Did the design of the product change during the design process?
  - How did he generate different options at each step of the design process?
- What is 3d printed and why? Why not use traditional manufacturing or standard components?
- Can end user or the community further build upon your product?
  - What can they change?
  - What can they build on?
- Business Thoughts
  - Why is your product better than others?
  - What is the current state and what are your future plans for the product?
  - Who is your target customer/user/community?
  - How does the product get adopted by the community?
  - What support does it get from the community?
  - How do you maintain quality standards?
- Manufacturing
  - How do you plan to manufacture this product in scale?
  - Technology monitoring: How do you do that?
  - Cost control. How do you do that

Annex B: Structure of Case Studies for Part II

Table 25: Structure of cases on User innovators and innovations

User Innovator
User need
Design Tools used
Artifact Created
Other Artifacts created
Collaborations
Modules of the product
Existing Interfaces
Designed Interfaces
Types of Interfaces
(1D/2D: computer systems,3 D: Mechanical Objects)
Modularity-in-use
Modularity-in-production
Modular operators used(Splitting, Substituting, Exclusion, Augmentation, inversion, Porting)
Cost
Comments on Modularity
Use of 3D printing
Process of user design
Suggestion from the network

Annex C: Survey Questions for Maker Event Participants

During the Academy

- How do you rate your technical expertise on a scale of 1-5 (very bad to very good)?
- How do you rate your business expertise on a scale of 1-5 (very bad to very good)?
- Do you have previous ICT experience? If yes, please state.
- Do you have previous startup experience? If yes, please describe in 2-3 lines.
- Did you have IoT or startup ideas before the academy start? If yes, please list up to three best ideas.
- What ideation tools or methods did you find useful during the workshop sessions?
- What idea do you currently find the most interesting and what do you like about your current idea?
- Describe (in three to four lines) how your idea reached its current state. Who and what inspired you, what decisions you made and why.
- What do you think of the pitch of your team? What are the positives and negatives?

After the Academy

- Describe (in three to four lines) how your idea reached its current state. Who and what inspired you, what decisions you made and why.
- What helped you understand and work with so many new technologies concepts during the short time at the academy?
- How did you decide on which tool to use (hardware/ software) from the choices you had (e.g. Edison, raspberry pi, Arduino, etc.)?
- Were the tools you used for hardware and software flexible enough for you to prototype innovatively and why?
- What other tools and gadgets would you have liked to work with during the IoT academy and why?
- What would be your ideal time-period and schedule to make something you feel is innovative and why?

Annex D: Survey used in Experiment

Questions/statements:

1. What is your gender?
2. I was able to design my own cupboard/shelf
3. The number of steps needed to design the cupboard/shelf is too high
4. The complexity of selecting an option is too high
5. The selection options and those effects on the final cupboard/shelf are clear
6. I need more variety to design my own cupboard/shelf
7. The final cupboard/shelf fits with my personal impression of a cupboard/shelf
8. I have specific requirements, and I know exactly what cupboard I want to design
9. The configurator supported me in finding a good solution
10. My personal idea of a good cupboard/shelf changed during the configuration process

Annex E: Glossary of Technologies and Organizations

3D printing	3D printing while currently refers to additive manufacturing in general originally referred to 'powder-bed' printing technology developed at MIT. The term "Three-Dimensional Printing" is a registered trademark of Z corporation (Grimm, 2004).
3D Printing services	Digital fabrication service that offers 3D printing. Please see digital fabrication services.
Actuators	Actuators convert signals into some physical action such as movement, heating, lighting, etc.
Arduino	The Arduino platform is an open source electronics platform based on easy-to-use hardware and software, aimed for anyone to make innovative projects (http://arduino.cc/ accessed on 2014-08-24)
Digital fabrication services	Digital fabrication services are provided by companies, which fabricate and ship to their customers. Examples include Shapeways, I.materialise, and Ponoko (https://www.ponoko.com/ accessed on 2015-12-17).
Drupal	A popular a free and open-source content management framework (https://www.drupal.org accessed on 2016-03-19).
Fused Deposition Modelling (FDM)	FDM prints from consumer 3D printers are in different types of thermoplastic, such as Acrylonitrile Butadiene Styrene (ABS) or Polylactic Acid (PLA).
General Public License	Stallman developed the General Public License or GPL (also referred to as "copyleft) where end users had the right to use it at no cost, to modify it, and to distribute modified or unmodified versions to others freely as long as it was not incorporated into commercialized closed source software.
I.materialise	"I.materialise" is a 3D printing service from Belgian company Materialise (https://i.materialise.com accessed on 2015-12-17).
Instructables	Instructables is an online community platform for sharing instructions or recipes for making and tinkering. It spun out of Squid Labs at the MIT. Media Lab (http://www.instructables.com/about accessed on 2016-02-12)
Internet of Things	Network of physical objects embedded with electronics, software, sensors to collect and exchange data.
Internet of Things Start-up Summer School	Internet of Things Start-up Summer School was conducted by Friedrich-Alexander University Erlangen-Nürnberg and UnternehmerTUM in Munich as part of STARTIFY7, a project funded by the European Union to promote entrepreneurship in ICT technologies. (http://startify7.eu/bavaria accessed on 2015-12-17).
JavaScript	JavaScript is a programming language essential to World Wide Web (www) content production, used in a majority of websites and supported by modern web browsers.
Laser Sintering	Laser Sintering is an additive manufacturing technique that uses laser to sinter and bond powdered material (often metal)

Lego Mindstorms	Lego Mindstorms is a kit that contains software and hardware parts to create customizable, programmable robots from the Lego group based in Denmark. The kit includes a computer to control the system, sensors, and motors along with Lego bricks that can be assembled to form robotics and other intelligent mechanical systems (http://mindstorms.lego.com accessed on 2015-12-17).
Lens-style Camera	Lens-style cameras are high-quality cameras that can be mounted to smartphones to take better pictures while reusing some of the smartphone hardware like the touch screen for its controls. http://www.sony.com/electronics/attachable-lens/t/lens-style-cameras accessed on 2015-12-17).
Littlebits	Littlebits is an open source library of modular electronics that snap together with magnets. It is used for prototyping and learning about basic electronic circuits http://littlebits.cc/ accessed on 2015-12-17).
LSI Logic	LSI Logic, (later LSI Corporation) was a semiconductor and software company founded in 1981 in California. In 2012, it had revenues of US $ 2.51 Billion. It was acquired by Avago Technologies in 2014 (http://www.sec.gov/Archives/edgar/data/703360/000119312513077227/d436577d1ok.htm accessed on 2015-12-17).
Makerbot	A New York City based company that produces FDM 3D printers like the Replicator series for end consumers (http://www.makerbot.com/ accessed on 2016-03-19).
Microcontrollers	Microcontrollers convert inputs from sensors into outputs for actuators based on a set of instructions programmed into them.
Nestlé S.A.	Nestlé S.A. is a Swiss multinational food and beverage company, formed in 1905. It is one of the world's largest companies with a market capitalization of US $247.3 Billion and revenues of $100.08 Billion in 2015 (Forbes, 2015).
Ninja Blocks	Ninja Blocks is an open hardware platform product with cloud enabled computers that have a variety of sensors and actuators, especially by controlling power sockets of other electrical appliances (https://ninjablocks.com accessed on 2015-12-17).
Online Public Access Catalog	OPAC is an online database of materials of a library or group of libraries.
Open source software	Open source software has its roots in the "free software" movement started by Richard Stallman in the early 1980s to counter the trend towards "closed" development of software. Its main feature is releasing the underlying source code of the software, which allowed other programmers to extend and reuse the software with little restrictions.
OpenSCAD	OpenSCAD is a free software application which converts text based design descriptions into 3D Computer-aided design (CAD) objects. The design descriptions are typically based on geometric shapes (http://www.openscad.org/ accessed on 2015-12-20).
Raspberry Pi	Raspberry Pi is a series of low-cost and credit card sized computers from the Raspberry Pi foundation based in the United Kingdom http://www.raspberrypi.org accessed on 2014-08-24).

Sensors	Sensors are objects that detect events or changes in their environment and send an electronic signal that can be further processed.
Shapeways	Shapeways is one of the pioneering 3D printing services founded in 2007 in the Netherlands. The headquarters is in New York (https://www.shapeways.com/ accessed on 2015-12-17).
Sims	Highly popular life-simulation video game series by Maxis
Soundcloud	Soundcloud is a social sound platform where users can create sounds and share them everywhere (https://soundcloud.com/pages/contact accessed on 2015-12-20)
Stata	Stata has data analysis and statistical software package.
Stereolithography (STL)	Stereolithography uses photo-polymerizing resin, which hardens to polymers.
STL file format	STL is a file format that was originally used for Stereolithography CAD designs but is now a format that is widely used for 3D printing. Popular backronyms are "Standard Triangle Language" and "Standard Tessellation Language" (Grimm, 2004).
Tessel	Tessel is a development platform that can be used to quickly prototype electronic products with Node.js that can later be optimized for manufacturing https://tessel.io/ accessed on 2015-12-27).
Thingiverse	Thingiverse is a 3D printing community, also for non-expert users. It is designed for discovering, making, and sharing 3D printable things http://www.thingiverse.com/ accessed on 2015-12-27).
Think.Make.Start	Think.Make.Start is a prototyping workshop for 14 days where participants can develop and build innovative products with inputs from experts from industry and research. It is conducted by UnternehmerTUM in their high-tech prototyping area MakerSpace (http://www.unternehmertum.de/thinkmakestart.html accessed on 2015-12-27).
Three.js	Three.js a WebGL based JavaScript library used to create and display animated 3D computer graphics on the web browser. More information can be found on its website (http://threejs.org/ accessed on, 2015-12-22).
Twine	Twine is a wireless sensor block with pluggable external sensors that can be used to monitor various data around the home and perform actions based on them http://supermechanical.com/twine/ accessed on 2015-12-19).
Voxel8	Voxel8 is a 3D electronics printer that prints in thermoplastics and conductive silver ink(http://www.voxel8.co/ accessed on 2016-03-19)
WebGL	WebGL is a JavaScript API for rendering interactive 3D computer graphics and 2D graphics within a compatible web browser. It is designed and maintained by the Khronos Group (https://www.khronos.org accessed on 2015-12-19).

MIX
Papier aus verantwortungsvollen Quellen
Paper from responsible sources
FSC® C105338

If you have any concerns about our products,
you can contact us on
ProductSafety@springernature.com

In case Publisher is established outside the EU,
the EU authorized representative is:
Springer Nature Customer Service Center GmbH
Europaplatz 3, 69115 Heidelberg, Germany

Printed by Libri Plureos GmbH
in Hamburg, Germany